Ultimate Parrot Guide

Linda S. Rubin

© T.F.H. Publications, Inc.

Distributed in the UNITED STATES to the Pet Trade by T.F.H. Publications, Inc., 1 TFH Plaza, Neptune City, NJ 07753; on the Internet at www.tfh.com; in CANADA by Rolf C. Hagen Inc., 3225 Sartelon St., Montreal, Quebec H4R 1E8; Pet Trade by H & L Pet Supplies Inc., 27 Kingston Crescent, Kitchener, Ontario N2B 2T6; in ENGLAND by T.F.H. Publications, P.O. Box 74, Havant PO9 5TT; in AUSTRALIA AND THE SOUTH PACIFIC by T.F.H. (Australia), Pty. Ltd., Box 149, Brookvale 2100 N.S.W., Australia; in NEW ZEALAND by Brooklands Aquarium Ltd., 5 McGiven Drive, New Plymouth, RD1 New Zealand; in SOUTH AFRICA by Rolf C. Hagen S.A. (PTY.) LTD., P.O. Box 201199, Durban North 4016, South Africa; in Japan by T.F.H. Publications. Published by T.F.H. Publications, Inc.

Manufactured in the
United States of America
by T.F.H. Publications, Inc.

Contents

Introduction 5

Selecting a Parrot 7

Choosing a Healthy Parrot 25

Cages and Equipment 33

Nutrition 41

Training and Taming 49

Behavior 55

Health Care 59

Resources 62

Index 63

Introduction

Selecting a parrot as a companion bird can bring much joy and happiness into your life, and when the choice is the correct one, your life will be richly rewarded. However, selecting the right parrot is not always an easy choice. There are many species of parrots, each with different personality traits, and there's no doubt that some varieties will fit into your lifestyle better than others.

It is your responsibility to provide a nutritious diet, a nurturing environment, and the time and attention that will keep your new companion bird happy and well adjusted. Chances are, if you do not provide these necessities for your bird, no one else will. There is nothing sadder than an unhappy parrot remaining locked in its cage, deprived of companionship because its owner was unable to understand its needs.

This book is dedicated to new companion bird owners and to all hobbyists who have experienced the special joy of keeping companion parrots, as well as those who are seeking to add additional birds to their aviary. The following chapters should provide considerable insight into the mysteries of parrot behavior, with information on how to select the right companion parrot, as well as advice on how to tame, train, house, feed, and provide the very best care so your new parrot lives a long and healthy life. Congratulations! You have brought a special new friend into your life; in return for your daily attention and gentle care you will receive much love, devotion, and affection from a truly extraordinary companion.

Selecting a Parrot

To be fair, the companion bird you choose should possess the characteristics that blend with your own personality so that both of you can live together in harmony. Choices made on impulse are not recommended. To make the right decision, you should read, study, and learn all you can about the species you intend to keep. The parrot you choose will depend solely on you for its daily care, upkeep, and all of its needs, so be certain your choice is made carefully so that your new bird receives the necessary attention it deserves.

If you have never owned a companion parrot before, it is generally recommended to start with one of the smaller species. A budgerigar (parakeet) or cockatiel makes an excellent first parrot, especially for families, children, and the elderly. For most parrot owners, they are the perfect and logical first choice. Once you understand and care for these wonderful, friendly little parrots, you may decide to try another small- or medium-size parrot. However, don't be fooled by size! Many of these birds are just as big in personality and as active as the large parrots, but with much less dangerous beaks should they throw a tantrum.

For most new owners, it can be disastrous to select a large bird such as an Amazon, cockatoo, or macaw as a first pet. Large birds generally require more of an investment in time and accommodations, not to mention the grocery bill. Also, large birds are usually much more costly, so study the different species carefully before you make a choice.

Another consideration before purchasing a parrot is to learn its age and find out its origin or source. For example, was it parent-reared, or was it handfed by the breeder at a younger age? This

As magnificent as it is, a Blue and Gold macaw may not be the right choice for everyone. Cost, size, and personality are just some of the factors to consider.

information will help determine how quickly you can tame the parrot. Older birds, especially those that may have had little contact with people, can be a challenge to tame even for the experienced owner.

You may also be interested in learning whether your parrot is male or female. As a general rule, most parrots are not sexually dimorphic, but must undergo either surgical sexing or DNA sexing procedures in order to determine their gender. There are, however, a few exceptions among some species. On the other hand, unless you intend to breed your parrot, it may not be necessary for you to know what gender it is.

It is also beneficial to find out if your bird has protective identification such as a permanent closed, coded, seamless leg band, or other means of providing proof that the bird is yours.

Finally, if you keep other birds, you will need to consider how you will introduce your new bird to your existing birds, and whether or not your new bird will be compatible with them. Any new bird acquired must also be properly quarantined before introducing it into the same environment of any existing birds you may have, which may be a further consideration.

When selecting a parrot for the first time, try to determine what characteristics you are searching for in a companion bird. Parrots have different natures: some are more independent, others have stronger personalities, while still others are more sedate. Similarly, some parrots are known for their singing and talking abilities, while others can scarcely utter a whisper-like "hello."

By learning a bird's personality traits before purchasing a parrot, you avoid being disappointed and losing interest in your new friend, a creature that is totally dependent upon you for care and companionship. The birds listed below are the species most available at this time in the pet trade. Rarer or infrequently seen species are not listed, although they can be sought out and found with some aviculturists, usually at a higher price.

Every bird has its own unique beauty. The key is to learn what you want in a companion bird ahead of time, so that you and your new friend can grow to appreciate and enjoy one another.

The Big Birds

The larger parrots are represented from each of the world's three major geographic distributions: Austral-Asia, Afro-Asia, and the New World. Although many parrots were once imported from the wild into the United States, most birds available today for the pet trade are captive-raised, mainly on bird farms and in aviaries by breeders and aviculturists.

When first considering a choice, usually the big parrots come to mind: African Greys, Amazons, cockatoos, and macaws. However, bigger is not always better. There are many other fascinating parrots from which to choose. But, if you appreciate the larger birds and have some experience with keeping other parrots, then there is nothing like the companionship of a large, feathered friend.

Amazon Parrots

Amazon parrots are New World parrots from Central and South America. They are predominantly green birds, with strong, engaging personalities and a playful nature. A common characteristic of the genus is their ability to raise their head feathers at the back of their neck presenting a larger, "hawk-headed" appearance. The more popular members include several of the large- and medium-size Amazons.

Among the larger species, the Yellow-naped Amazon, *Amazona ochrocephala auropalliata,* and Double Yellow-headed Amazon, *A. o. oratrix,* are the most frequently available. The Yellow-naped is a predominantly green bird, with a blaze of deep yellow on the nape of its neck that "colors out" or broadens with maturity and is absent on young birds. The Double Yellow-head has a green body and carries a brilliant yellow head with bright yellow adorning the shoulders and leggings, with red mixed on the shoulders. The Yellow-headed Amazon does not color out fully until maturity, and it may take a number of years before its head becomes fully yellow.

Both the Yellow-naped and Yellow-headed Amazons are outgoing, playful species that are unsurpassed for their singing ability and may mimic opera, arias, and other sounds. Along with the Blue-fronted Amazon, *A. aestiva,* they can make excellent talkers. Their propensity for clarity and tone, as well as their ability to amass large vocabularies, make them popular favorites, although the Blue-fronted can have a softer voice. Many individuals of these species are known for becoming attached to one person in the household, sometimes behaving aggressively toward anyone else who attempts to feed or handle the bird. Unfortunately, it is impossible to predict these individuals ahead of time.

Once tame, some of the medium-size Amazons such as the Red-lored, *A. autumnalis,* and the Orange-winged, *A. amazonica,* are usually willing to interact with more than one person, although again, there can be exceptions. The Red-lored is one of the most colorful varieties, its head marked with vivid red on the lores (the area between the eyes and the beak), lavender feathers on the crown, and yellow cheeks. As the parrot ages, the yellow intensifies and blends into the red lores, resembling a beautiful orange sunset. The author once had an otherwise quiet Red-lored Amazon that learned to cluck like a rooster and on occasion would sing the full chorus.

The Blue-fronted and Orange-winged are often confused, but an easy way to tell the difference is that the Blue-fronted is larger and has a solid black beak. Some of the Blue-front subspecies vary in the amount of yellow and blue

Amazons are some of the larger parrots from which to choose as a pet; some Blue-fronteds make good talkers.

Cockatoos, such as this Lesser Sulfur-crested, typically enjoy cuddling; however, their screams can be unbearable.

on the face, and the most striking variety is known as the Yellow-winged Amazon, named for the extensive mix of yellow, with a dab of red on its shoulders. The Orange-winged is a smaller bird with a deeper blue on the face that runs onto the crown, with a horn and black beak, and orange feathers replacing the usual red wing speculum that other Amazons have. Among the Amazons, only the smaller White-fronted Amazon, *A. albifrons*, is sexually dimorphic.

Because Amazon parrots can scream and engage in loud squawking or other deafening noises, apartment and condo owners might wish to reconsider such a choice. This is not to say that every Amazon is a screamer, but many can be loud and can be encouraged by other birds or circumstances they find stimulating.

Although Amazon parrots are considered one of the most difficult genera to reproduce in captivity, they can form close bonds to others of their own species as well as outside of their own genera. The author had a Lilacine Amazon, *A. a. lilacinae*, which in the absence of a suitable partner formed a close bond with an Indian Ringneck parakeet, *Psittacula krameri manillensis*. The Lilacine Amazon would hold its foot up in the air for minutes at a time, and with obvious enjoyment allow the Indian Ringneck parakeet to gently preen its toenails.

Amazons can be quite independent and can be left alone for periods of time to amuse themselves, but they should be provided with plenty of toys to satisfy their need to chew and keep them occupied. Their major drawback is a fierce temperament when undergoing hormonal changes during breeding season; they'll bite even their owner. Amazon-proof toys, even wooden nest boxes for chewing, can be appreciated at this time. It is best to keep other family members and pets out of reach during this stage, which will pass once hormone levels return to normal.

Amazon parrots are an excellent choice for those who desire an intelligent, charming, playful bird that's a smart thinker and that enjoys attention and companionship. Even tame Amazons can bite, so they are not recommended for young children.

Cockatoos

Cockatoos inhabit countries within the Austral-Asian distribution and are uniquely impressive with their long, recumbent crests and engaging personalities. The large white cockatoos are among the most popular species of the cockatoo family. These grandiose, majestic birds include the Sulphur-crested cockatoo, *Cacatua galerita*, the Moluccan cockatoo, *C. moluccensis*, and the Umbrella cockatoo, *C. alba*.

The Sulphur-crested is about 20 inches long, all white, with a sulphur-yellow erectile crest and a slight tinge of yellow on the undersides of the wings and tail.

The Moluccan cockatoo, due to its shorter tail and broader white feathers, gives the appearance of being the largest of the white cockatoos. This is especially apparent when the recumbent pink crest is raised, revealing a vivid flash of deep salmon-pink underneath. Some individuals have a more pronounced pink wash, especially on the chest. The white tail is tinged with yellow. The Umbrella cockatoo is all white, with a yellow tinge under the tail and wings.

There are five species of the smaller popular white cockatoos. The Lesser Sulphur-crested cockatoo, *C. sulphurea sulphurea*, is a smaller version of the Greater Sulphur-crested cockatoo with a yellow tinge on the breast and cheeks. The Citron cockatoo, *C. s. citrinocristata*, is beautifully adorned by its citron-orange crest. The Goffin's cockatoo, *C. goffini*, is the smallest and perhaps the sweetest, with a shorter crest and tinge of red on the cheeks. And, the Bare-eyed cockatoo, *C. pastinator sanguinea*, known as one of the most intelligent cockatoos, has the characteristic blue naked skin patch below the eye.

The two pink species of cockatoos that are usually more expensive are the Rose-breasted cockatoo, or Galah, *Cacatua roseicapilla*, and the Leadbeater or Major Mitchell's cockatoo, *C. leadbeateri*. To many, these are two of the most beautiful members of the cockatoo family. The Galah is predominantly silvery gray with a rose-pink face, breast, and abdomen. There are two subspecies with subtle differences in the depth of pink coloration, shape of crest, and skin color around the eye.

The Major Mitchell's cockatoo is perhaps the most striking of all cockatoos. It is predominantly white on the back, wings, and tail, with soft pink shading the chest, abdomen, neck, chin, and face. The crest is unique, with three bands of color: red on each side, a yellow center, and tipped in white. Some aviculturists believe there may be two other subspecies with minor differences in color.

A cockatoo is the best choice for those with prior bird keeping experience who wish to keep a species they can hold and cuddle. Once tame or handfed, cockatoos relish being held and stroked, many enjoy extensive stroking under the wing—an action many Amazon parrots would not tolerate—at least not to the same extent as a cockatoo would allow. Unlike some Amazons, they are not great talkers, but they can be taught to speak, and their screams can go beyond deafening, especially in the larger species.

Some cockatoos can become very dependent and closely bonded with their human companion, so it is best to set up a routine schedule right from the start. Spending an entire week with a cockatoo to tame it, then going off to work and leaving the bird alone a large part of the day can be extremely frustrating to some birds and could cause such negative behaviors as screaming and feather-plucking. Umbrella and Moluccan cockatoos in particular are noted for their tantrums and destructive behavior if not trained correctly. A normal schedule from the start, so the new arrival knows what to expect, and the addition of a variety of toys changed every so often to prevent boredom, will help get these companions settled into a familiar routine.

Cockatoos require a large cage, and because they are big chewers they also need an abundance of toys, branches, and wood to keep them occupied. While outside the cage, cockatoos enjoy perching on playstands and some can be taught to "dance" or naturally assume dramatic postures, much to their owner's, and their own, amusement.

Macaws

The three genera of macaws are from the New World distribution. Although the large macaws are impressive in size and color, they are not for everyone. Macaws require sufficient room with large accommodations, along with plenty of time and attention from their keepers. These majestic

The charismatic Severe macaw, one of four mini-macaws, may be a good choice for those who don't have room for a larger parrot.

beauties require macaw-size caging to accommodate their lengthy tails, so be prepared to purchase the largest cage you can afford to keep them in when you're not able to be around.

With their massive beaks, macaws require plenty of wood or special macaw-size toys to occupy them, as they will otherwise reduce most wood to its tiniest splinter form. Always provide plenty of suitable toys to satisfy their natural need for chewing.

Macaws can be extremely loud when they wish to be. When kept as pairs, they can be deafening, encouraging each other with their boisterous, noisy episodes. However, some macaws kept as single pets behave quite well and are suitable for condo or apartment living, providing they are given daily exercise outside the cage. In general, their ability to speak clearly is not rated very high, although there are exceptions and many can acquire large vocabularies.

In many ways macaws are like Amazons and cockatoos. Some tend to be temperamental and nippy at times; others can be gentle and sweet, even wishing to be cuddled like some cockatoos. Macaw pairs bond very closely and can live for many decades.

Some of the larger, popular macaws include the Scarlet, Green-winged, Blue and Gold, Military, and Hyacinth.

The Scarlet Macaw, *Ara macao,* is nearly three feet long, half of which is a long, tapering tail. It is the most vivid of the popular macaws, colored scarlet throughout the body, which is more brilliant on the head, with extensive yellow and blue coloring the wings. A paler blue colors the rump, and the tail is red mixed with deeper shades of blue. The eye patches on the face are white. Scarlet Macaws can vary in temperament. Some individuals adore cuddling, while others can become nippy at times.

Green-winged macaws, *A. chloroptera*, are often confused with the Scarlet macaw, but this species is distinguishable by its easily observable pattern of red feathers on the facial patch, dark green feathers replacing yellow on the wings, and its deeper red body color. The flight and tail feathers are blue, and the tail is tipped with deep red. Some Green-wings develop large, although noisy, vocabularies.

Blue and Gold Macaws, *A. ararauana*, are a combination of rich, deep blue on the neck, back, wings, and tail, with golden yellow coloring the underparts. The crown is tinged with green and the face carries rows of tiny black feathers across the fleshy-white cheek patch. A black collar frames the chin area meeting the throat. This species is known for its intelligence, mischievousness, and ability to talk with a clear speaking voice.

Military macaws, *A. militaris,* are olive-green, with deep red on the forehead, tiny black feathers lining the bare facial patch, and bluish-red primary flight feathers. Its shorter tail—making it appear smaller than the scarlet—is a brownish-red with the underside shaded olive-yellow. The Military, which is usually less expensive than the other large macaws, is known for its loud voice and fair ability to talk.

Hyacinth macaws, *Anodorhynchus hyacinthinus,* are the largest of all parrots, about 34 inches long, and one of the most expensive. Their color is a rich, glossy blue throughout, with a bright yellow naked skin patch surrounding the eye and framing the lower mandible. Its black, massive beak makes it a powerful chewer and it should be provided with the toughest of hard woods for perches and toys. When acquired at a young age, Hyacinth macaws can make fair talkers, and they enjoy cuddling and playing.

A young Congo African Grey has great potential for speaking; some Greys can even mimic a ringing telephone or a barking dog.

Because Hyacinths are the largest of the macaws, they can take extra time to wean. Be certain any Hyacinth macaw you are considering is fully independent and eating on its own before accepting the bird.

Although there are two other species in the genus, the Glaucous macaw, *A. glaucus,* and Lear's macaws, *A. leari,* both are rare, smaller, and paler versions of the Hyacinth. Due to the efforts of dedicated aviculturists who specialize in the species, Hyacinths are being bred in enough numbers that some are available for the pet trade. However, like a growing number of other parrots, Hyacinths are endangered in the wild, which is why breeding such birds in captivity is important.

Mini-Macaws

If you like the look of the larger macaws, but do not have the available room, select one of the several species of mini-macaws. Because their shorter tails allow them to be kept in smaller cages, they make good companions for apartment living. Yet, these dwarf macaws are quite active and playful, so they should be given a spacious cage in addition to time outside in order to adequately exercise.

These smaller versions of the large macaws, once tamed, make good family pets and can become fair talkers. Although they can be loud, single pets bonded to their owners are generally less noisy.

They have strong, powerful beaks for chewing, and like the larger macaws need plenty of sturdy toys to amuse themselves.

There are four species of mini-macaws, each ranging from 14 to 20 inches in total length, including a long tapering tail: the Severe, *Ara severa*, which resembles the Military macaw; the Yellow-collared or Yellow-naped, *A. auricollis*, with its distinguished yellow collar; the colorful Illiger's or Hahn's, *A. maracana*, which resembles a large Halfmoon or Petz conure *(Aratinga canicularis eburnirostrum);* and the smallest macaw, the Noble, *A nobilis*, which closely resembles the Blue-crown conure, *(Aratinga acuticaudata)*.

African Greys

Rated as perhaps the very best talker of the entire parrot family, and possibly second in the bird world only to Mynahs, the African Grey makes up for its less colorful appearance through its keen intelligence and outstanding ability to talk. Greys can mimic, to exacting perfection, human voices, household noises, and most any sound they hear.

Some birds can be taught to associate sounds with events. For example, it is not uncommon for a Grey to mimic the sound of the telephone ringing, answer it with a "hello," and present a one-sided conversation. One Grey belonging to the author's friend was taught to hold onto the side of its swing while swinging violently back and forth, and yell with enthusiasm "Ride 'em cowboy!"

Perhaps the most famous African Grey, known as "Alex," was taught by Dr. Irene Pepperberg to amass a vocabulary of several hundred words and further amazed non-believers with his word association to objects and events. For example, when asked to pick up a red square block Alex was able to do so with ease; trials were all varied with new tasks so that he could not rely simply upon memorization.

Eclectus parrots have unusual feathering and stunning coloration: males are green with red, and females are red with deep blue.

Selecting a Parrot

Though individuals do vary, some African Greys are known to be high strung and very sensitive and may not do well in busy, confusing households.

The Congo African Grey, *Psittacus erithacus*, is gray throughout and has a bright red tail. The subspecies known as the Timneh African Grey, *P.e. timneh*, is darker gray, with a maroon tail, and is slightly smaller. Although the Timneh does not have quite the reputation of talking ability as the Congo, it can still learn a sizable vocabulary, and it must be remembered that individuals of any species can and do vary.

Eclectus Parrots

One of the few sexually dimorphic parrots, the Eclectus, is easily sexed. Males are colored a brilliant green with red side patches on the body, a black lower mandible, and a yellow-orange upper mandible. Females

Lories and lorikeets, such as these Rainbow lorikeets, may require extra cleaning and maintenance because of their special nectar diets.

are stunning in brilliant red with a deep blue coloring the nape, abdomen, and underwings, and an entirely black beak. The feather quality of Eclectus differ from other parrots in that it almost resembles finely brushed fur, and parrot show standards at exhibitions allow for this unique difference.

There are nearly a dozen subspecies of Eclectus. In females, some of the variations reveal lighter blue on the chest, an eye-ring finely lined in blue, and some yellow or orange-tipped tail feathers. The nominate race is known as the Grand Eclectus, *Eclectus roratus roratus*; the three subspecies more popularly available are the Solomon Island Eclectus, *E. r. solomonensis*; the Red-sided Eclectus, *E. r. polychloros*; and the Vosmaeri Eclectus, *E. r. vosmaeri*.

Known as sensitive birds, especially the females, they are very gentle when tamed and can learn to be fair talkers with reasonably clear voices. Due to their sensitivity, they also fare better in quieter households. Bonded birds enjoy interaction with their owners and sharing their company. Eclectus should be housed in large cages with plenty of toys made of soft woods for their softer beaks to be able to chew.

Medium-Size Parrots

Some of the more popular, moderate-size parrots include genera from each of the three geographic regions parrots inhabit around the world. Medium-size parrots from Austral-Asia include lories and lorikeets, rosellas, and the long-tailed Australian parrots. The Afro-Asian distribution includes the *Pocicephalus* species and *Psittacula* parakeets. And, from the New World distribution: pionus, conures, caiques, and Quaker parakeets.

Lories and Lorikeets

Among the lories and lorikeets, the Rainbow lorikeet, *Trichoglossus haematodus*, is the largest of Australia's lorikeets and one of the most colorful. Also seen, among others, are Dusky, *Pseudeos fuscata*; Goldie's, *T. goldiei*; Chattering, *Lorrius garrulous*; and Red, *Eos bornea*. In general, those that have shorter square tails are called lories; those with long, tapering tails are called lorikeets.

Lories and lorikeets are brilliantly colored and are extremely entertaining, active birds, fond of engaging in acrobatics. They make playful pets once tame, and can learn to talk fairly well. As nectar feeders, they have specific dietary requirements that must be met, including daily clean-up, as they tend to shoot their dropping due to their more liquid diet.

Rosellas

Rosellas are quiet, colorful Australian parrots that some compare in temperament and shape to that of overgrown budgies. They should be kept in large cages because, like budgies, they can become aggressive when stressed by too many birds to one cage. However, as single pets they are quite affectionate, and although they have limited vocabularies they can be taught to whistle tunes exceptionally well. The most available include the Golden Mantled or Eastern rosella, *Platycercus eximius*; Stanley or Western rosella, *P. icterotis*; and the Crimson rosella, *P. elegans*.

Australian Parakeets

Australian parakeets vary a great deal in size. Species commonly available range from the larger Rock Pebbler (Regent parrot), *Polytelis anthopeplus*, graduating down in size to the Baraband (Superb parrot), *P. swainsonii*, and the Princess of Wales, *P. alexandrae*; to the smaller Red-rump, *Psephoyus haematonoyus*, and Bourke's, *Neophema bourkii*. These graceful, elegant birds dressed in pastel shades make gentle companions. Although they don't enjoy cuddling, handfed birds are gentle and interactive. The smaller species such as the Red-rump and Bourke's can live harmoniously

The Crimson rosella, like others of its kind, should be given plenty of living space to prevent aggressiveness.

with other non-aggressive birds such as cockatiels and doves, providing all are given plenty of space and access to feed and water.

Cockatiels

Another small, popular Australian parrot is the cockatiel, *Nymphicus hollandicus*, which is almost a miniature version of the larger white cockatoo with its recumbent crest. In fact, the cockatiel is considered by some as the link between the larger parakeets and the large white cockatoos. The sole member of its genus, cockatiels are plentiful in captivity and are available in a growing plethora of mutations, including lutino, pied, cinnamon, pearl, and whiteface, as well as their numerous cross-mutations. Rarer colors can be found with breeders who specialize in these mutations.

Cockatiels make excellent first small parrots, and are wonderful family pets and companions when handfed, especially for children and senior citizens. They enjoy sitting on household members' shoulders, having their nape and crest feathers gently caressed, and interacting with family members. Although the cockatiel's voice is not as clear as the larger parrots, both sexes can be taught to speak a number of words; males excel especially at whistling. Their voices, though high-pitched, are not as loud as larger parrots, so they can make excellent companions for apartment dwellers.

Pastel coloring and a gentle nature characterize the lovely Princess of Wales parakeet.

The cockatiel, a small and friendly parrot, is a popular first choice for families; the birds also come in many color mutations.

Cockatiels can be the swiftest flyers of the parrot family, and for that reason their wings should always remain clipped to prevent their escape, especially if there is any chance of a forgotten open window or the unexpected event of the front door opening. In order to effectively slow down cockatiels, the flight feathers on both wings should be clipped. Leaving the outer two or three primary feathers can help break a fall, although strong flyers or wilder birds may need these outer feathers trimmed as well.

Cockatiels require a parrot cage with bar spacing for cockatiels to prevent them from accidentally

The Jardine parrot is the largest and perhaps the most extroverted of the Poicephalus *genus, which also includes the Senegal, Meyers, and Red-bellied.*

catching their heads between the bars of a larger cage. Similarly, the cage grid at the bottom of the cage should be removed if there is any chance a cockatiel could catch its head there while reaching through to retrieve a fallen item.

Cockatiels are unaggressive, friendly birds that are unable to defend themselves even against smaller species. They must be kept separate from other species, even smaller more aggressive birds that may harass them or monopolize the food and water bowls. Cockatiels enjoy an assortment of toys made of soft woods and other safe materials.

Poicephalus

Of the African species, the *Poicephalus* genus offers several species that are popular favorites, including the Senegal, *P. senegalus*, and the Meyers, *P. meyeri*. Less commonly found *Poicephalus* include the Cape, *P. robustus*; the Red-bellied, *P. rufiverntris*; the Brown-head, *P. cryptoxanthus*; and the largest of the genus, the Jardine, *P. gulielmi*. Although they are tinted in muted shades of browns and greens, they also carry some bright dabs of yellow, orange, or red somewhere on the body. But what they may lack in color, they more than make up for in their charming personalities.

Poicephalus parrots are known for their shy, yet sweet dispositions, with a keen ability to learn tricks and learn how to talk. Although their voices are not as clear or as loud as the larger parrots, they still must be taught not to scream while young. When trained, they make a perfect small parrot for apartment and condo living, and although they enjoy a variety of toys and playstands, they are independent enough to occupy themselves when their companions can't be around. They require parrot cages with narrow bar spacing and plenty of room. Like many of the shyer species, they should be socialized to a variety of situations while young to make them better adjusted and people-oriented.

Psittacula

The genus *Psittacula* contains a number of large, graceful parakeets tinted in pastel shades with colorful rings encircling their necks. These regal parakeets are a soft pastel green, with long tapering tails, and nearly all the males have red beaks. The more popular species are the rose-ring parakeets, the African Ringneck, *P. krameri krameri,* and its subspecies the Indian Ringneck parakeet, *P. k. manillensis.*

The Indian Ringneck comes in an ever-growing number of color mutations, some extremely expensive due to their rarity. The more available color mutations from breeders include lutino,

Selecting a Parrot

> ### Helpful Hint
>
> Due to their popularity in aviculture and as pets, there are a great number of books available on budgerigars, cockatiels, lovebirds, and many other species of parrots. When you have narrowed down your choice, select a book that is devoted entirely to that species to provide you with additional information and insight. The additional knowledge you will gain will more than outweigh the cost of the book.

blue, albino, gray, gray-green, and cinnamon; a myriad of rarer colors and their combinations exist with specialist breeders.

The Moustache parakeet, *P. alexandri,* has eight subspecies, of which only two are available.

Novices easily confuse three *Psittacula* species: Plumhead parakeets, *P. cyanocephala;* the less common Blossom-head, *P. rosa,* which has more muted shades; and the Slateyhead, *P. himalayana,* with more subdued body color and a darker slate-gray head. They are only slightly smaller than cockatiels and require cages with cockatiel bar-spacing to prevent their escape or their heads from becoming caught.

One of the two largest members of the genus, the Alexandrine, *P. eupatria,* known also as the Greater Rose-ringed parakeet, has a top-heavy appearance due to its larger, disproportional beak, but it is balanced out by its unusually long tail. The Derbyan, *P. derbiana,* is nearly as large as the Alexandrine; all *Psittacula* species chew, but Derbyans especially are known to be powerful chewers and loud vocalizers. Both Derbyans and Alexandrines require large, strong, parrot cages.

Handfed *Psittacula* species can make excellent pets, but it is important to continue daily handling in order to keep them tame, especially while young. If time lapses between handling, it usually takes only repeated handling a few times a day to bring them back to their former tameness. Many can acquire an extended vocabulary if properly taught to talk. Although their voice is not as loud as the larger parrots, it is clearer than that of a cockatiel or a smaller bird.

Psittacula species all need wood to chew, and the larger species appreciate hardy toys, plain wood, and extra branches to strip.

Pionus

The *Pionus* are a genus from the New World distribution of Central and South America known for their calm, quiet, and gentle nature. They can be shy birds but learn to interact with people through proper training. Some are the size of the smallest Amazon parrots, such as the White-fronted Amazon, *A. albifrons albifrons.* Like Amazons, *Pionus* can have a more independent nature that does not require your

The aptly named Moustache parakeet sports a blackish facial mustache on its grayish head.

The Pionus parrots (White-capped shown) share some characteristics of the Amazons, including an independent nature and breeding season moodiness.

constant attention, yet like Amazons, they also demonstrate mood swings during breeding season until hormone levels return to normal.

Pionus parrots have soft voices, so they are not the best talkers, but that can make them a perfect choice for apartment or condo lifestyles. In general, they are not big chewers, but they do require parrot size caging and toys to keep them occupied. Some of the most available *Pionus* species include the Blue-headed (Red Vented), *P. menstruus;* White-capped, *P. senilis;* Maximilian's, *P. maximiliani;* Dusky, *P. fuscus;* and Bronze-wing, *P. chalcopterus.*

Conures

Conures have long slender bodies, large heads and beaks, and long tapering tails. In appearance they look like miniature versions of the larger macaws. In fact, some of the largest conures are bigger than some of the mini-macaws.

Conures can be distinguished from macaws by their smaller eye-rings and lack of a bare, facial skin patch. They come in a wide variety of colors and sizes. Species that are commonly available are from the genus *Aratinga,* known for its brighter colors and ear-splitting vocalizations in close quarters, and the genus *Pyrrhura,* which are not quite as colorful but are much quieter.

If handfed or tamed while young, *Aratingas* make excellent, affectionate, playful pets. Their noisy voices can be coached to amass a fair vocabulary if taught while young. They have wonderful personalities, develop strong bonds with their owners, and do well in either calm or busy households. Because of their more powerful voice or raucous screams, they may not be the best selection if neighbors object to noise, especially if birds are acquired as untamed adults.

Conures require attention and interaction, and like other parrots, may scream their objections if they do not get it. They should be given a large parrot cage with plenty of room and enough toys to keep them busy.

Popular *Aratinga* species include the smaller, colorful yellow-red-green Sun conures, *A. solstitialis,* and the nearly as colorful Jenday, *A. jandaya.* Larger available species include the Red-headed, *A. erythrogenys;* the Blue-crowned, *A. acuticaudata;* and the Queen of Bavaria, *A. guarouba.* The latter is a brilliant yellow with deep green flight feathers. It is the largest, just over 14 inches long, very expensive, and one of the most highly prized.

Popular *Pyrrhura* species include the White-eared, *P. leucotis,* and the Maroon-bellied, *P. frontalis.* The *Pyrrhuras* have the same attributes of the noisier *Aratingas,* but their quieter voice may make them better suited to apartment living if noise is a consideration.

Another large and popular conure is the Nanday, *Nandayas nenday,* the sole member of its genus. The Nanday is closer in appearance to *Aratingas*, and its voice is just as loud. It is primarily green with a black head and bright red thighs. Like many conures, it is also considered to be very intelligent.

Caiques

Although there are possibly five species in the genus, only two are available in the pet trade. The White-breasted, or White-bellied, *Pionites leucogaster,* is primarily green on the back, off-white on the breast, with apricot-orange coloring the face down to the shoulders. The subspecies, the Yellow-thighed, *P. l. xanthomeria,* has yellow thighs instead of green. The Black-headed, *Pionites melanocephala,* varies from the White-breasted by its distinctive black cap, eye-ring, feet, and beak.

The Sun conure, one of the most popular of the conures, is noted for its playful personality and bright coloration.

These 9-inch comical little clowns are extremely inquisitive and intelligent. When handfed, they make playful companions that are animated and that will thrive with family attention. Their voice is somewhat loud and they are not good talkers; however, their personality greatly makes up for any lack.

Like lories, caiques can be playful acrobatics, learning headstands and other tricks. They need a large cage with plenty of toys, and like other active parrots, they should always be supervised when playing outside their cage so they don't end up in trouble. Caiques enjoy bathing frequently, which contributes to their high-gloss plumage, and they should be allowed access to a shallow dish of water in which to bathe.

Quaker Parakeets

The Quaker or Monk parakeet, *Myiopsitta monachus,* is a slender, 11-inch South American parakeet colored light gray on the face and underparts and a soft green around the eyes, nape, back, wings, rump, thighs, and long tail.

In the wild they build communal nests, and some owners claim that providing a nest box will calm their territorial aggression. Handfed babies make affectionate, lively companions, and they are considered intelligent and good talkers. They require a spacious parrot cage and plenty of toys, wood, and branches to satisfy their natural chewing and nest-building instincts.

Brotogeris

The more commonly available species are

> **Helpful Hint**
>
> The distinguishing feature between a parrot and a parakeet is tail and body shape: parrots have short, square body shapes and tails, whereas parakeets have long, slender body shapes with long tapering tails. That description also applies to the budgie, because as a long-tailed bird it does qualify as a parakeet.

Canary-winged, or Bee Bee, parakeets, *B. versicolurus*, and Grey-cheeked parakeets, *B. pyrrhopterus*. They are primarily green birds with accents of yellow or gray, respectively, and are about 8 inches long. These birds make excellent companions; they enjoy riding their owner's shoulders and hiding in clothing and pockets. Their antics can get them in trouble and they can be aggressive with other birds. They have loud voices and some do learn to talk. They require cockatiel bar-size caging, with sturdy toys that hold up to inquisitive beaks.

The Smallest Parrots

For parrot-size personality wrapped in small packages, the major contenders include African lovebirds, South American parrotlets, and the well-known Australian budgerigar or shell parakeet. These smart little parrots are known for their brazenness and often behave as if they don't realize how small they really are!

Like budgerigars, the common species of lovebirds are well established in aviculture. The most available species and their mutations include the Peachface, *Agapornis roseicollis*, and the Masked lovebirds, *A. personata*. There are almost as many color mutations in Peachface lovebirds as there are in budgerigars. Aviculturists do keep other rarer species of lovebirds and are careful not to hybridize them.

Unfortunately, lovebirds don't always live up to their name, and some species, especially Peachface, can be extremely pugnacious toward other birds, including other lovebird species, and therefore should never be caged with them. Because lovebirds need continuous interaction to remain tame pets, it is recommended to acquire a handfed baby, which will simplify training. As to their talking ability, their voices can be sharp and their natural sounds can be too shrill for some tastes.

Lovebirds are another example of a nest-building parrot, and they will often prefer to sleep in a nest box or similar structure at night. They will often tear up materials such as the paper lining the bottom of their cage, which they tuck in their rump feathers to bring back to their "nest." They require cockatiel or budgerigar bar-size caging, toys and swings, and they enjoy frolicking on playstands when outside the cage.

Parrotlets are the South American counterpart of the African lovebird and the smallest of all parrots.

Inquisitive and fearless, handreared Black-headed caiques make delightful companions.

They are primarily bright green, with limited blue accents. They are known to be bold, bossy, and mischievous, and have a reputation for believing they are a large parrot! Parrotlets tend to be argumentative and aggressive with other birds, even other parrotlets. They require budgie cage-bar spacing, and toys to keep them busy. When trained they can learn how to talk and do a variety of tricks. Their voices are more diminutive to match their size, so they make ideal pets for apartment or condo lifestyles.

Although there are seven species of parrotlets, the more popular species are Pacific, or

Selecting a Parrot

Celestial, parrotlets, *Forpus coelestis,* about 5 to 6 inches in size; Spectacled parrotlets, *F. conspicillatus;* and Green-rumped parrotlets, *F. passerinus.* Pacific parrotlets are being bred by aviculturists in a number of growing color mutations that include lutino, blue, albino, fallow, and American yellow. Green-rumps are known to have more gentle dispositions and are a good choice for children.

The most popular pet bird in more than 6 million U.S. households is the budgerigar, *Melopsittacus undulates,* better known in the United States as the parakeet. Its true name is budgerigar in its native Australia, or "budgie" for short, and it is in actuality only one of many species of parakeets from the different geographic distributions around the world.

Although Quakers can be excellent pets, the prolific birds are restricted in some states because of their reputation as agricultural pests.

Budgies make fantastic first pet parrots. They are engaging, entertaining, and charming companions. They can be taught to perform tricks, and although their smaller voice is mechanical in sound, they can learn hundreds of words. Their size varies between pet stock size and exhibition (or English) show size, and some are bred together to increase the size of their pet stock. Either variety make good pets, and their noisy chatter is so musical and pleasant, with occasional softer squawks (compared to most parrots), that they are perfect apartment pets.

It is important to obtain young just weaned babies, as close to 38 to 42 days old if possible, because it makes training then extremely simple. Budgies are so amenable to training that it is rarely necessary to hand-feed. Budgies enjoy interacting with their owners and can be kept with other budgies once tamed.

At 9 inches long, the Canary-winged parakeet is relatively small, but it packs a giant, fun-filled personality.

Choosing a Healthy Parrot

After you have researched and selected the species that best meets your personality and lifestyle, your next step is to choose a healthy bird. Healthy parrots resonate with energy and vitality, they are alert and interested in their environment, and they are responsive to other birds and people.

A parrot's health is reflected in its outward appearance and feather condition. Feathers should be clean, tight, and held close to the body. There should be no sign of soiled, damaged, or fluffed-out feathers. Missing feathers, abnormal feathers, or bare spots on the body can indicate serious illness or feather-plucking behavior, both of which should be avoided.

When a parrot is in peak condition its feathers are immaculate. Bird show judges refer to this state as being in top condition. A bird in perfect feather condition radiates good health, which is why the category of condition is a major component of parrot show standards. A wing clip is one of the permissible exceptions to perfect feather condition.

Hard and Soft Molts

All parrots molt or shed feathers from time to time; for example, when they molt from baby feather into juvenile plumage, or go through their annual adult molt. Tiny pinfeathers may emerge on the head and nape, some small body feathers may be molted, or a few missing flight or tail feathers may be found at the bottom of the cage. There is no need for concern because these feathers are dropped so they may gradually be replaced with new ones. This normal process is known as a soft molt. When too many feathers have fallen out all at once, or a bird is smothered in pinfeathers, it indicates an abnormal condition or hard molt. Hard molts may arise from a number of problems, including environmental, behavioral, and physiological causes. For example, parrots

When selecting a parrot as a pet, take time to look at the bird and where it lives—its surroundings should be clean of debris and droppings.

may be thrown into a hard molt due to sudden increased temperatures, new stressful conditions that break with routine, or as a result of disease. Parrots that are undergoing a hard molt should have their diets supplemented with additional protein at this time to help build new feathers.

Signs of Illness

Symptoms of ill health in parrots include sluggish, listless, depressed behavior, as well as decreased appetite, usually accompanied by fluffed-up body feathers in an attempt to stay warm. Some birds will tuck their beak into the feathers on their back, although this should not be confused with routine afternoon naps taken late in the day. Birds with advanced respiratory ailments will often sit low on the perch, with eyes closed, beak gaping, and tail pumping, which indicates labored breathing. There may also be sneezing, wheezing, and discharge from the eyes, beak, or nares (nostrils). Another red flag or warning sign to illness is a "pasty" vent, or droppings clinging to a bird's vent and surrounding feathers.

Before making a purchase, carefully examine the bird's environment to observe whether conditions are clean and if other birds appear healthy. A number of food and water vessels should be present and recently filled with a variety of foods, including some fresh produce. All surfaces, including feed vessels, perches, and toys, should be free of droppings, regurgitated material, and foreign matter.

A parrot's droppings are an indicator of health and a guide to what it has been eating. Normal droppings are round, semi-solid, either green or black, with a white urate center. They should

Choosing a Healthy Parrot

not appear discolored, overly loose, surrounded by a wet water ring, or contain blood. Bright green droppings or droppings that contain blood require immediate medical attention.

A bird's diet and nutritional schedule can affect its droppings. For example, fresh fruit and green food may temporarily cause droppings to be runny until a bird adjusts to the new diet. Also, provisions of fresh produce on an infrequent schedule, when a bird is not accustomed to fruits and vegetables, can contribute to the same problem. Pellets, or extruded products, can change the color of the droppings to brown or to the same color as the pellets. Because a bird drinks more water on a pelleted diet, its droppings tend to be looser than when fed an all-seed diet.

Frequent handling of your pet may help to alert you to subtle signs of illness, such as weight loss or labored breathing.

Before purchasing a parrot, it is best to find an experienced breeder or handler to weigh the parrot or feel its breastbone. The breastbone, or keel, should not feel too sharp to the touch, and the chest should feel "meaty" on either side. Underweight birds will not feel "filled out," and overweight birds will feel "fatty," or plump. Unfortunately, new owners can be fooled by parrots they thought were "fat and sassy," but were only hiding a thinner physique under many layers of feathers. An experienced handler of the species will be able to feel the difference.

A more accurate method of obtaining a bird's weight is to arrange a full veterinary exam with a certified avian veterinarian who specializes in birds. An avian veterinary specialist will be able to weigh the parrot and determine what is an appropriate weight for its species. Although pet shops and breeders vary in their return policies, many will agree to a veterinary exam with the option to return the bird. However, always obtain any health guarantees in writing and never assume anything without first finding out your options.

By selecting a healthy bird, your new parrot will have a better chance of tolerating a stressful move, adjusting to a new environment, and bonding with its new owner.

Helpful Hint

Because birds in the wild are easy prey when they show symptoms of illness, they are adept at hiding their symptoms. For bird owners, this means that there may be no symptoms until a bird is extremely ill. Parrots sitting listlessly at the bottom of the cage can be very sick birds and will require immediate medical attention.

Identification

Today there are three methods available to provide permanent identification for parrots: closed coded bands, microchips, and tattoos. Permanent identification is important not only as a consideration to theft, but also as a means of protecting the safety of a special companion. For example, because the federal Wild Bird Conservation Act no longer allows the

Fluffed-up feathers on a lethargic bird are an indication that something may be wrong; consult with your veterinarian as soon as possible.

mass importation of parrots from the wild into the United States, it is becoming important to adequately demonstrate that a bird is captive bred. In addition, other situations such as airline travel and show exhibition could require parrots to be marked as proof of ownership, origin, or to validate health certificates and vaccinations.

The most popular method used for identifying parrots is closed banding chicks with a traceable, aluminum, seamless leg band. At the appropriate age, the band is gently slipped over the first two or three toes and the remaining toes are pulled through. The chick can only be banded by a certain age, generally ranging from 7 to 21 days, depending upon the species. The correct age for banding is usually determined by when the chick's eyes begin to open and when the toes have grown large enough so the band can't slip back off. If this time window is missed, it is usually too late to band the chick. Therefore, closed banding with a coded, aluminum, seamless leg band is one way to prove that a breeder raised a bird.

Bands purchased through one of the national parrot organizations will usually carry three or four letters indicating the organization's initials, letters and/or numbers representing the breeder's code, the current year, and a number that indicates which parrot was bred by the breeder for that year.

Closed banding with a traceable band allows the owner to contact the band secretary of that organization and locate the breeder through the band code. The breeder could then look up the number imprinted on the band to find that bird's personal file. The history contained in that file might include information on genetic origins, family bloodlines, pedigrees or show information, and any history of illness or of treatments prescribed.

Some birds wear aluminum closed bands that are not traceable unless the breeder is already known. The band may only carry the breeder's code, year, and a number signifying which bird was banded that year. This type of band is only

Helpful Hint

Once you bring your new parrot home, closely monitor the number, size, and consistency of its droppings. Observing the droppings over a 24-hour period will tell you what your parrot has been eating, how much it has eaten, and how it is feeling. Any large deviation in the number and appearance of droppings may indicate a health or adjustment problem. Although new birds do require a settling-in period, in general, small parrots with their higher metabolisms may have as many as 20 droppings in a 24-hour period; larger parrots will have fewer, depending upon their size. New owners should learn what is considered normal for their bird, so they can learn to recognize signs of illness and take action.

useful to the breeder to keep track of his own stock. Some of the smaller parrots might wear what is known as family bands or colored bands, which mark birds from different bloodlines so a breeder can distinguish them at a glance.

The only drawback to relying on a leg band for permanent identification is that a leg band can be removed. There are also some rare cases where a leg band may become too small as the bird grows if the correct size is not chosen, or swelling may occur if some foreign material becomes lodged and irritates the foot. Should there be swelling in either instance, the band would have to be removed by a veterinarian using band cutters.

Though microchips and tattoos are now being used more frequently for identification purposes, a traditional closed band is still the method of choice for many.

Another identification method now gaining in popularity is the use of microchips. Microchips are very tiny chips inserted by an avian veterinarian with an instrument designed to place them just below the skin. These chips can be read by a specific device and can provide positive proof that the bird is registered to its owner.

The third method of permanent identification is to have a qualified avian veterinarian place a special tattoo under the wing. Should a leg band need to be removed, either microchipping or tattooing a bird could be considered.

Weaning

It is understandable that most new owners will want to select a parrot that is young enough to train, a situation that often translates into buying a handfed baby. Although handfed parrots are desirable pets, be absolutely certain that the one you select is completely weaned and eating on its own, especially if this is your first time as a parrot owner. Weaned baby parrots, handfed or not, are able to eat entirely on their own and live in a separate cage apart from their parents.

Unfortunately, there are many heartbreaking stories about unweaned baby parrots that were taken home before they were weaned because a well-meaning new owner thought they could finish feeding the chick. Because they were unskilled or inexperienced in handfeeding techniques, much to the owner's dismay, the baby aspirated and died (a common tragedy occurs when formula is erroneously pumped down the windpipe instead of the esophagus, as well as when a chick is overfed). Other common stories tell of frustrated owners who are forced to continue handfeeding for several months beyond normal weaning time, because they unknowingly reinforced the parrot's begging behavior, or quit feeding a chick too early and lost the chick.

Even with experience, feeders should be given detailed information on every aspect of the babies in their care. This includes how to prepare formula and how often to feed, the precise feeding instructions naming all materials used, the exact formula recipe (and formula samples) or name of the commercial preparation, and several handfeeding demonstrations by the breeder. Only after several

All birds should go through a period of quarantine—of at least 30 days—before being introduced to the rest of your feathered friends.

successful feeding trials should the chick be released into the care of the new owner.

Some breeders who are anxious to sell a parrot to lighten their own handfeeding schedule, or just to be able to sell what they have available, may sell an unweaned baby at a reduced price. In general, responsible aviculturists do not condone this practice unless the buyer is also an experienced aviculturist. However, even experienced breeders have been known to lose chicks. And size is not always an issue in handfeeding. Because of their digestive systems, cockatiels and cockatoos can be some of the most challenging species to hand-feed. It is often said that if you are able to successfully hand-feed a cockatiel, you could hand-feed most any other parrot. However, it is worth spending more to acquire a fully weaned parrot that is ready to go to a new home equipped with a good head start on life.

In reality, handfeeding does not guarantee the tameness of a parrot. Rather, the art of gentle handling, the method of feeding, and the age of the chick will have greater bearing on its tameness. Young parrots, newly weaned from parent-raised stock, lovingly handled and used to people, can also be tamed. Conversely, handfed parrots that are not treated with tender loving care, or that are not regularly handled, may have to be tamed again.

Quarantine

If you own other birds you must quarantine any new arrival for a minimum period of 30 days. The ideal quarantine period is 60 days, or even 90 days should illness be discovered. Quarantine is necessary to protect your new bird and your existing birds from catching or spreading disease.

Ideally, quarantine should take place at a separate facility and in isolation from other birds. Should you need to quarantine a new bird at home, try to keep the quarantined bird on a separate air system or at least in a separate room. Better yet, board the bird with a close neighbor, friend, or relative, and visit each day to observe the bird and see to its needs.

During the period of quarantine, never allow another bird to visit the quarantined bird or land near or on its cage. Always feed and water your existing birds first, then see to the needs of any birds under quarantine. After servicing

Helpful Hint

Handfeeding is a serious commitment and an art that requires practice. It is very easy to overfeed and aspirate a baby that is screaming noisily and is eager to be fed. Only experienced feeders should attempt handfeeding.

quarantined birds, change out of your clothes, shower, and put on fresh clothes before you interact with your other birds.

Quarantine can be a useful period of adjustment for a new parrot. It allows you to introduce or convert a bird to a new diet, observe your bird's behavior, and get to know your bird before you starting training in earnest. If a bird is healthy, then once it has settled in there is no reason not to proceed with some taming techniques. However, should symptoms of illness surface, it is better to treat the parrot according to your veterinarian's instructions and not stress the bird further by postponing training sessions. There is no need to keep visits brief, however. Let your bird get to know you. Be sensitive to its mood, and talk to it in calm, soothing tones. Let your bird learn to associate you with positive occurrences such as bringing tasty food, keeping it company, and showing affection in a non-threatening manner.

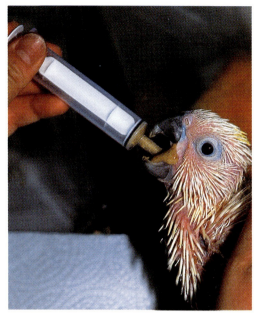

Handfeeding is a very technical procedure that should only be done by those with experience; serious harm—even death—can result from improper techniques.

If you have an expensive collection of birds or special companion parrots you wish to safeguard, have your new parrot tested by your avian veterinarian before leaving quarantine and placing it in the same room with other birds.

Should illness be found and tests prove positive, you will have to begin the quarantine period again and treat the bird with the prescribed medications. Always finish all medication as directed and retest any bird proven ill, even if the bird appears recovered, before introducing it into the collection or exposing it to another bird. This precaution is necessary because sick birds are able to hide many symptoms of disease, and testing is the only safe means of protecting other birds. The time and expense involved in testing a new bird far outweighs the cost and heartache of medicating and possibly losing your other birds.

Cages and Equipment

There are some excellent parrot cages and a full line of related equipment available on the market today. Cages range in a wide variety of sizes and materials, and just about any model can be found in most retail stores today. Custom cages may be ordered from distributors through the numerous bird catalogs that may be obtained from advertisers in pet bird magazines and bird organization newsletters. Due to market demand there are now a number of specialty parrot products available to companion bird owners—parrot playpens, tabletop stands, carriers, custom cage covers, toys, ladders, swings—any of which can help pamper a pet parrot.

Cages

Choosing a cage for your new parrot is an important decision. Never purchase a cage without first considering the needs of your new companion.

First and foremost, have a clear idea which species you will be buying, then shop specifically for a cage that will house that species in comfort. If you intend to buy a big bird such as a cockatoo or Amazon, you will need to purchase one of the largest cages; this item should be considered as part of the total cost of your new bird. If your choice is a macaw, then chances are you will be purchasing one of the biggest and most expensive cages to accommodate the size of the bird, especially its lengthy tail. Smaller species have specific needs, too. Be certain to purchase cages that have narrower bar spacing for the small and medium size birds that require it: cockatiels, lovebirds, parrotlets, budgies, larger parakeets, and others that might escape or injure themselves in a typical parrot-size cage.

Cages come in a wide variety of shapes, sizes, and styles; choose one that suits your particular needs and is easy to clean.

Another point to consider before selecting a new cage is the amount of time your new bird will be spending in it. Will your bird need to stay inside while you are at work all day? Or will you be able to supervise your bird outside the cage at home most days? Even if you allow your parrot considerable freedom, you may still wish to offer it the largest cage you can afford in the event that you one day acquire a companion for your bird.

Be certain that the cage you select is sturdy and does not easily come unlocked or fall apart, especially during times of transport. Many a sad story has been heard about cages accidentally dropped, or those that have fallen apart in the owner's hands because latches were not securely fastened or were easily disengaged.

Whichever cage you choose, be certain it is safe for your bird without being a security risk, that it contains no hazardous edges, and that it can be easily cleaned and disinfected. If your parrot is an escape artist, find a padlock to prevent him from opening the door. However, always keep the key in plain sight in the event of an emergency such as fire, flood, or earthquake.

Select materials appropriate for the species you keep. Some materials such as brass and chrome are strong and durable. These materials are easy to clean with hot water, completely disinfect, and will last many years. There are a number of other sturdy cages available that hold up well for many species. Be careful to avoid inappropriate materials such as bamboo or weak plastics, which any self-respecting parrot can easily chew through to freedom.

Be certain there is plenty of space for perches so your bird can move around comfortably in the cage. Offer natural tree branches such as eucalyptus, willow, apple, beech, maple, and harder woods such as manzanita for big chewers like Amazons, cockatoos, and macaws. Avoid cherry branches, which are toxic to parrots. Parrots enjoy stripping the bark off of branches and they derive minerals from the bark in the process. Always wash all perches thoroughly to remove pesticides and any foreign material. And remember, your parrot frequently uses his perch as his "napkin" to wipe his beak, so be certain to clean all perches often. Finally, vary the perch size by offering perches of varying diameter to provide exercise for your parrot's feet and to prevent foot problems from developing.

When selecting a cage, consider its construction and the materials used. If you are ordering a large aviary or using galvanized wire, make certain it is thoroughly scrubbed with a brush and washed with vinegar to remove any trace of zinc residue that could lead to zinc toxicity and poison your bird. Cages using cheaper wire are even more dangerous because the galvanized coating is easier for a parrot to chew off.

Symptoms of zinc toxicity include regurgitation, diarrhea, weakness, lethargy, weight loss, seizures, and death. Emergency treatment is necessary; a number of medications are administered that move the metal through the gastrointestinal tract and excrete the zinc through the kidneys. A high fiber diet and additional treatment for several weeks may be necessary depending upon the severity of the poisoning and how much zinc was ingested. Prevention is the best protection.

A well-equipped cage makes a happy home for your pet, especially if it has plenty of toys and perches—perhaps even a play area on top.

Covering the Cage

Some parrots feel more secure when their cage is covered for the night. A covered cage provides privacy and shields a bird from any drafts that might lead to illness. It also provides a dark environment that is more conducive to restful and undisturbed sleep.

Covering the cage at bedtime can act as a signal to a parrot to quiet down for the night and stop chattering or vocalizing. As that time approaches, a parrot may start to settle in, roosting for the night ahead, grinding its beak in anticipation of being covered up for the night. Parrots can be like people, they function better when they go to sleep on a schedule at the same time every night; a good night's sleep can be a jumpstart to the immune system for any living creature.

The appropriate cage cover depends mainly upon temperature and climatic conditions. In cold climates it may be necessary to use towels over which a blanket can be placed for added insulation. In warmer climates or seasons, a thin towel can be used. In hot temperatures, a light sheet, or perhaps a cover on only the back, sides, and top of the cage (leaving the front open for better ventilation) may be all that is necessary. For those with designer tastes, custom cage covers can be ordered from some manufacturers, in some cases featuring the bird's name.

Be certain that toys are safe and durable enough to stand up to your inquisitive bird's powerful beak.

Sometimes, covering the cage can prevent night fright, a condition in which a bird is startled by an unexpected sound or light, such as when a car's headlights shine through a window into a bird's cage. If the bird thrashes around in its cage, however, it may be best to turn on the light for a few minutes until the bird settles down again. Usually, after a few minutes, a bird will calm down and can be covered up again.

There are some exceptions to when a parrot's cage should be covered. For example, when a bird has been deeply traumatized and is fearful of having its cage covered—perhaps reminding it of being captured or being wrapped in a towel for frequent medications. In this situation it may be better to discontinue covering the cage. If it is tolerated, try leaving a towel around the back and partly on the top and sides of the cage to provide some security. Otherwise, wait until you have tamed the bird and completely won its trust before reintroducing the act of covering the cage. If covering the cage continues to be a source of trauma, then you may have to abandon the effort.

However, once you do cover the cage, continue to do so every night. Should you choose to stop, wait until warm weather so your bird does not catch a chill.

Playstands, Jungle Gyms, and Bird Toys

There are a number of excellent playstands, gyms, and toys on the market. Make certain all materials are safe, and only purchase items that lend themselves to easy cleaning and disinfecting procedures.

Most parrots enjoy entertaining themselves on a playground, and they are highly recommended. Playgrounds can also be used for training sessions; therefore, those equipped with casters can be rolled to other areas of the house to allow you to continue supervising your bird while it is outside the cage (tabletop versions can serve the same purpose). If you have several parrots, you may need to invest in more than one stand to prevent territorial battles, injuries, or the possibility of spreading infection to others if a bird has been ill. Some stands do not contain wood but allow you to change or provide your own perches, or use other materials that can be disinfected. Because wood is porous, it cannot be completely disinfected like other materials.

When choosing toys, select only those made with safe materials such as plain wood (or woods dyed with natural food coloring), rawhide, or other similar materials. Read the label carefully. Check all toys with bells or chain links to make certain they are safe, completely closed, and not a threat to your parrot. Many parrots enjoy bells because they have a "cause and effect" relationship (the parrot can affect its environment by actively ringing the bell), and they can become a special favorite. Try to find toy bells with wood, rawhide, rope, or plastic without chain links that might be opened by strong beaks.

Another point to consider when selecting toys is to determine if the size of the toy is appropriate for the species it is intended to entertain. Most toys are labeled, but use common sense. Scrutinize the various parts of the toy, including any plastic pieces that might become detached and swallowed or stuck in a bird's throat. Another danger lies in chain links large enough to trap a small bird's head, where it may become stuck and a parrot may, in panic, be strangled. Be careful using any type of clips to attach items to a cage. If they must be used, have the sharp edges facing toward the outside of the cage where a bird's tongue or face cannot be caught. Always use a version of Murphy's Law when caring for birds: "If you think it won't happen, it usually does."

Bird Carriers and Acrylic Cages

One of the most useful conveniences has been the "discovery" of bird carriers, also known as dog and cat kennels. The carriers work well for transporting birds to the veterinarian, as well as for visits and other travels. Be certain, however, that the carrier is completely secure and is resistant to opening should it fall to the ground. Also check that the door can be latched securely. A towel or small blanket helps to keep the bird warm and shielded from drafts in cold weather. A light sheet or pillowcase can be used during warmer months; this covering not only shields the bird from drafts, but also provides security from all the strange sights and sounds during transport.

The kennel carrier may not be able to be accommodated on airlines when you wish to fly with a pet under your seat. In these cases you will have to purchase a small animal carrier that meets individual airline regulations. They are easy to find and cost about the same as dog and cat kennels. It is helpful to attach

Travel carriers provide a safe and comfortable means of transport as well as a way to protect your bird from the elements.

Perches, toys, and other cage accessories should be regularly disinfected; however, those made of porous wood may need to be discarded.

several perches, such as the manzanita branches that attach by hardware, plus several food cups from which to perch and eat. Don't fill the water dish while traveling; it will only splash around and make a mess. Instead include a slice of orange for moisture and don't forget to add spray millet—a treat most birds cannot refuse.

Acrylic cages have the advantage of shielding a bird from drafts while allowing others to look in. Many breeders use them to either exhibit their parrots at shows or bring birds to meetings and fairs to sell. They are now catching on with parrot owners who use them for transporting their pets. Additional advantages to acrylic cages are that they are easy to clean, can be used as a brooder, or even made into a hospital cage if necessary.

Cleaning and Disinfecting

Be consistent in cleaning your parrot's cage. Good hygiene is important to your bird's health. Droppings, old food, and other materials allowed to collect or turn bad can harbor bacteria and pose a disease risk. Change the cage paper each morning when you refill dishes, change drinking water, and offer fresh produce.

Always wash your hands thoroughly between handling food items and cleaning or serving other bird's cages. Not enough can be said for the excellent and sensible practice of washing hands with old-fashioned soap and water. Do so frequently and thoroughly to protect your parrot from coming in contact with bacterial organisms. If you are treating a sick bird, you can obtain iodine surgical scrub from your veterinary pharmacy to wash your hands between or after servicing any sick birds.

Any perches that become dirty should be scraped with a perch cleaner, knife, or scissors, washed and disinfected before returning to the cage. Better yet, use natural tree branches, which can be replaced when dirty. Cement

Helpful Hint

Good hygiene is always the best prevention to disease. Only give your parrot clean dishes that you would consider drinking out of yourself. Scrub water cups thoroughly every day and refill with fresh, clean drinking water. Be sure to clean thoroughly and remove any buildup of foreign matter that collects in corners.

Cages and Equipment

perches, in addition to being rough on a bird's feet, are not always easy to disinfect. Sandpaper perches are unnecessary. Parrots do not need gravel to digest their food; their gizzard churns up their food for them.

Always have an appropriate disinfectant on hand to clean cages, food cups, toys, playstands, carriers, and other accessories. Wash items in hot, soapy water; rinse well, then spray with the disinfectant. Read labels carefully and follow the directions. Most will state that all surfaces must remain wet for the duration of 10 minutes in order to be effective. If the surface dries in less than the time allowed, you must spray again. To find an appropriate disinfectant, locate a distributor of bird products that advertises in any of the birds magazines, or ask your local pet store or veterinary clinic to order one for you.

It is a good idea to keep a second set of feed cups and water vessels to switch to when the current cups are dirty. Scrub items first in hot, soapy water to remove any foreign matter, then either run through the dishwasher, spray with disinfectant, or soak them for 20 minutes in a bucket containing a gallon of water and a quarter cup of bleach. Make sure to rinse and dry thoroughly before storing.

Nutrition

Proper nutrition, in combination with good hygiene and health practices, is one of the major strengths in fighting off and combating disease. Unfortunately, most avian veterinarians still find malnutrition, a forerunner of disease, to be a major medical problem among their patients. However, a number of feed manufacturers have found a growing maket and are attempting to satisfy consumers' needs by conducting more nutritional research geared to parrots, rather than relying on poultry studies. This has brought about a growing number of convenience foods and products high in nutrition. In addition to improved seed mixes, the formulation of pelleted products, and special "people food" cook-and-serve diets, there are a vast variety of treats and specialty diets available. These diets, rounded out with fresh fruits and vegetables, as well as clean fresh drinking water, keep parrots healthy and give them a greater chance to live a long life.

Seed Mixes, Pellets, and Extruded Diets

Although seeds can be a supplementary part of the diet, an all-seed diet for parrots is not the most nutritional menu and can even contribute to malnutrition. In the wild, most parrots don't come in contact with many of the seeds we offer them in captivity. They move from crop to crop, or field to field, eating whatever is available, thereby receiving a varied diet.

Good nutrition is a major factor in ensuring a long and healthy life for your companion parrot.

Most parrots in the wild never encounter sunflower seeds. The only problem with parrots eating sunflower seed is that they eat too many. Sunflower is both high in protein and fat, and when fed as a key component of the diet, it is much too fattening and is therefore unhealthy. On the other hand, sunflower seed fed in moderation or on occasion has value. Similarly, safflower seed is another high-fat seed; although it is a better quality fat, it still has fat. Unfortunately, safflower is lower in protein than sunflower, so owners substituting safflower seed for sunflower are not doing their parrots any favors.

Because seed is deficient in most vitamins, with the exception of some of the vitamin B complex group, manufacturers have fortified seed mixes with added vitamins and minerals. This process is generally done in either one of two ways. One method is to open the seeds and impregnate them with the additional nutrients. This can possibly expose the seeds to bacteria, although the heating process is presumed to eliminate any chance of contamination. The second method is to add a pellet that contains the nutrients to the seed mix, but the problem remains as to whether the parrot is actually ingesting them.

On the positive side, many of the seed mixes available today are fortified with dehydrated fruits and vegetables, as well as other nutrients, to give a parrot a better nutritional menu. However, many mixes still remain high in sunflower or safflower as the basic component, and an owner can only guess if other items in the mix are being eaten.

Based on nutritional studies, manufacturers have in recent years developed pelleted or extruded diets that meet the nutritional needs of parrots, as is best understood at this time. The claim is that pellets or granules contain 100 percent of all nutrients in each particle consumed. Also, there is less waste because there are no leftover seed hulls.

Pellets or extruded diets are available in granules, crumbles, and pellets. Companies go to great lengths to make pellets both palatable and attractive to parrots by manufacturing them in a variety of sizes, shapes, and colors. Inquisitive parrots pick them up to play, accidentally taste them, and eventually learn to eat them. Pelleted and extruded diets are available at pet stores or through distributors. Some distributors even sell samples so your parrot can discover the brand it prefers.

Some companies also manufacture species-specific or prescription diets. Some of these formulations include high-protein diets, low-fat diets, calcium-enriched diets, lory diets containing fructose, and breeder diets. Medicated diets are also available through your avian veterinarian.

To convert your parrot to pellets or an extruded diet, follow the manufacturer's instructions on the label very closely. Parrots vary—some will convert right away, while others will take much

Nutrition

longer. Some companies recommend a slow conversion by mixing the pellets half-and-half with your parrot's regular diet and increasing the amount of the new diet over a few weeks until the bird is converted. Others recommend a fast conversion by removing the bird's normal diet and offering the pellets for one or two days, but returning the parrot to its regular diet if necessary and trying again in a few days. It is critical to closely watch your parrot so that it does not starve should it refuse a new diet. Some birds, like cockatiels, are creatures of habit, and other parrots can be stubborn too. Be certain your bird goes to bed with a full crop at night, as parrots cannot go more than a day without food.

Although this baby African Grey's dietary needs differ from an adult's, it still requires a varied menu that includes fresh fruit and vegetables.

Other Nutritional Snacks

Parrots also benefit from some of the cook-and-serve "people foods" that are microwaveable and packaged for birds. These packages include ingredients such as corn, rice, bean mixes, exotic fruit and nut mixes, pasta and vegetables mixes, all of which provide added nutrition.

Another favorite is panicum millet or millet spray. This is actually millet seed cut while still on the stock and is relished by most parrots. Bigger parrots may also enjoy the larger size millet that is available. Spray millet is one food that many birds eat even when they are feeling ill and refuse other foods offered.

Other treats available include nutritional items such as bird cakes and bird berries, which can be fed in limited amounts daily. However, other more fattening treats should be fed only occasionally, as long as they do not contribute to excessive weight gain.

Fruits and Vegetables

Feeding a variety of fresh fruits and vegetables on a daily basis can add tremendous nutritional impact to your parrot's menu and can challenge curious, busy beaks to remain active and content. Although you may choose to feed a pelleted or extruded diet, manufacturers often recommend supplementing with fresh fruits and vegetables as a means of providing additional tastes and textures that are psychologically satisfying.

Because many seed diets are deficient in vitamins, and because some parrots pick out only the seeds they like and ignore other ingredients, many parrots seen today by avian veterinarians are suffering from malnutrition. Additionally, parrots that engage in feather-picking activities are usually found to have underlying illness, an inadequate environment, even malnutrition. Adding fresh produce to the menu can have a profound effect, stimulating a parrot to play and interact with its

A pelleted or extruded diet may make up the bulk of your parrot's calories, but different foods, textures, and tastes will hold a bird's interest.

environment, boosting its nutritional intake to combat malnutrition, and strengthening a parrot's immune system so it can fight off disease.

Because vitamin A is a common deficiency found in parrots, the best fruits and vegetables to select are those with the highest amounts of antioxidants, particularly the beta-carotenes that can be converted into vitamin A in the liver. The smartest plan is to offer a wide variety of fruits and vegetables while selecting at least one vegetable high in vitamin A each day. Choose from raw, dark green, leafy vegetables and the red-orange-yellow vegetables that are all high in carotene.

Raw, dark greens highest in vitamin A (listed in their descending order) include dandelion greens (including the flower), carrot tops, collard greens, kale, comfrey, and spinach. Also, broccoli, mustard greens, turnip greens, Swiss chard, beet top, chicory, escarole, parsley, and watercress, while not high in vitamin A, do have other antioxidants that are valuable. Avoid light-colored greens such as lettuce and cabbages, which are composed primarily of water and have very little food value.

Vegetables high in vitamin A (listed in descending order) include cooked yams, carrots, red pepper, and cooked pumpkin, squash, and sweet potato. Because carrots are inexpensive and very high in vitamin A, many breeders feed them to their birds by the pound. For convenience, mini-carrots can be purchased at many supermarkets and do not require peeling. Just wash and serve. Avocado is poisonous to birds and should never be offered. Although corn is greatly relished by parrots, it lacks many vitamins; however, it is an excellent source of fiber in the diet. Most parrots enjoy holding a one-inch wedge of corn on the cob to eat. Corn is an excellent soft food for young birds, breeding birds, and birds that are too ill to crack harder seed.

Many breeders and parrot enthusiasts offer a mix of cooked corn, whole grain rice, and cooked beans for added nutrition. For an easy snack offer a corn, rice, and bean diet in the following manner. Cook whole grain brown rice in advance and store it in the refrigerator (it can also be frozen in small portions). Purchase a dry bean mix, cook according to instructions, and store in separate packages in the freezer. Or, buy canned, cooked beans such as kidney beans, black beans, lima beans, pinto beans, split peas, or chickpeas, etc. Keep a package of frozen capped corn or corn "niblets" in the freezer. To prepare, microwave a serving of frozen corn and beans, then add the rice from the refrigerator (or microwave from the freezer) and mix until warm. Be careful to check the temperature for any hot spots in the center before offering to your bird.

Another easy to prepare alternative is to mix whole grain rice in a serving of fresh frozen cooked vegetables and corn. Add canned beans or legumes and you have a protein meal with a side of vegetables for your parrot.

Just about any fruit can be fed to parrots, although the exotic yellow-orange-red varieties such as papaya, mango, and cantaloupe are highest in vitamin A. Other favorites include apples, oranges, pears, tangerines, pomegranates (parrots adore the seeds), nectarines, peaches, plums, lemons, limes, blueberries, strawberries, blackberries, raspberries, cherries, honeydew, and others. A special favorite of *Psittacula* species is dried figs cut in quarters; birds will jealously hold the pieces with one foot and eat with great gusto, as they would devour a fresh fig in the wild. With the exception of papaya, pomegranate, and apple, do not feed any other seeds or pits because they can be toxic. Cherry pits are also known to be poisonous to birds.

Whatever produce you choose to buy—organic, store bought, or garden grown—be certain to wash it thoroughly to remove any traces of pesticides or other foreign substances. Soak fruits and vegetables separately in a clean bowl of water while frequently rinsing. The abrasive action of holding items under running water and thoroughly rinsing to remove residues is more effective than just soaking alone. Be careful not to soak fruits or vegetables any longer than five minutes because valuable vitamins can be lost.

Table Food

Any food that is good for you is good for your parrot. Think of your parrot as a health food nut. Never feed chocolate (which is toxic to birds), sugar, alcohol, caffeine, or tobacco, as these items can prove deadly to parrots. You can supplement the diet with additional quality proteins such as scrambled or hard-boiled eggs; well-cooked, deboned fish, chicken, and meat; or peanut butter sparingly spread on whole wheat bread. Pancakes, French toast, and whole grain breads can be offered as a treat but be certain to read the label to avoid any breads that contain chocolate or caffeine. Other selections from the carbohydrate group include pastas, noodles, rice, macaroni, etc., all without the sauces. Be aware that carbohydrates can prove fattening, so as with most foods, feed these items in moderation.

Always remove any leftover fresh foods at bedtime or by the next morning and replenish with fresh. Because eggs can gather bacteria within a few hours, it is wise to remove all traces of egg food if the bird hasn't consumed it within three hours.

An added benefit to feeding the corn, rice, and bean diet, or any of the table foods or soft foods mentioned above, is that should your bird become sick or too weak to eat harder pellets or seeds, it can survive by eating softer foods supplemented with vitamins.

Vitamin and Mineral Supplementation

Most birds can't resist spray millet; however, it should be used as a treat, not as the major part of a diet.

In general, additional vitamin and mineral supplementation is not necessary if you are feeding your parrot a pelleted or extruded diet along with fresh fruits and vegetables. However, if you are using a seed mix, even a fortified brand with added vitamins, you cannot be certain that it is being eaten; therefore, added vitamins are usually recommended. One easy method is to fill a salt shaker with the vitamin and give a light "salting" of the vitamin on the daily ration of fruits and vegetables, on the corn, rice, and bean mix, or on any other fresh or table foods your bird enjoys eating. Be certain to select a vitamin that contains vitamin D_3, because vitamin D_2 cannot be absorbed by birds. Also, find one that contains minerals and electrolytes to be certain your parrot is receiving everything it needs.

Calcium

The major mineral all parrots need is calcium, which is available in several appealing forms to parrots, either as traditional cuttlefish bone or as a mineral block. Cuttlebone can be easier to eat for smaller species with smaller beaks. To catch their interest, scratch some ridges across the surface and make sure the soft side is facing inside the cage.

Today, mineral blocks come in designer colors with added nutrients; these tend to stand up to strong beaks that might crush a cuttlebone in a blink of an eye. Although cuttlebone is fine to feed to even the largest macaws, owners sometimes panic when the cuttlebone is destroyed. However, consider that the object is to get the bird to eat the calcium. Therefore, if the parrot ingests it, the goal is achieved.

Water

Fresh, clean water must be provided on a daily basis to safeguard your parrot's overall good health. If the water from your area is not healthy enough to drink, consider buying a faucet filter or bottled water for your bird. If you need to use bottled water, use it to clean the water cup and refill it, so there is no risk of contamination.

Special Dietary Needs

It is now becoming known that different species of parrots vary in their dietary needs. For example, African Greys require additional calcium in their diets; Eclectus parrots have an increased need for vitamin A along with daily fresh fruit; and conures require vitamin K, which aids in blood clotting abilities. Consult your avian veterinarian or the Association of Avian Veterinarians (see

Nutrition

Resources) for precise dosages. Among the small parrots, budgerigars are prone to developing goiter and therefore require iodine. You can obtain an iodine solution for budgies from your veterinary pharmacy to use as a prophylactic in the water once a week.

Some species are affected by how much fat is in their diet. Rose-breasted cockatoos are prone to growing fatty tumors and should be fed an extremely low-fat diet. Pelleted diets are best at 2 to 5 percent fat content. If seed is fed, use a budgie mix. Eliminate sunflower or safflower seeds. Offer nutrition cakes or berries daily in limited quantities and lots of fresh greens and vegetables everyday.

Amazon parrots and other cockatoos are also prone to gaining weight. Pelleted diets are best at low to moderate fat levels (up to 5 to 6 percent). If seeds are fed, be stingy with sunflower and safflower.

Conversely, macaws require a diet higher in fat content. Large macaws such as Hyacinths eat palm nuts in the wild for their extra fat. Look for a fat content of 10 percent in feed mixes or consult your avian veterinarian for species-specific diets.

With their brush-like tongues, lories and lorikeets require a special diet of nectar made fresh each day in addition to lots of fruit. Some products are available that are species specific for this genus. Consider the extra nutritional care of a lory before purchasing one.

Some species also vary in their protein requirements. Published research from the University of California at Davis Psittacine Research Project found that cockatiels should be maintained on a dietary level of protein not higher than 15 percent, which could be increased to 20 percent while breeding. The amount of fat should also be lower for nonbreeding cockatiels, but can be increased slightly during the breeding cycle.

Training Parrots To Eat New Foods

In order to accept and eat new foods, birds need to be exposed to them on a daily basis. Exposure while young is very important, and the first few weeks can be critical to forming good eating habits. However, even older birds can be converted. Try presenting new foods in different shapes, sizes, and positions inside and on top of the cage. Some birds love to roll around in fresh, dripping wet greens as if to take a bath before eating. Others like to hold them while they munch; still others are enticed when greens are clipped to the side of the cage with a wooden clothespin or threaded through a feed cup. It can take months to train a bird, so owners should be prepared for some wasted foods until the bird begins to experiment with them. The time and effort, however, is well worth it because these foods provide both excellent nutrition and a source of play and amusement for your parrot.

Helpful Hint

If you already have one trained bird, it sometimes helps to use this bird as a "teacher" to train your parrot to eat new foods. Place the teacher bird within easy viewing range and offer the new foods to both birds. More often than not, the new bird will watch the teacher bird and will sample the item just to find out what it is missing. It may take several trials before your new parrot is chomping merrily away so do not be discouraged. Once it learns to eat new foods, it will be easier to entice it to eat other foods in the future.

Training and Taming

The process of training and taming is essential because it creates a loving bond that is built on trust, companionship, and mutual respect. Lacking training, your bird could stay wild and headed toward the unhappy possibility of remaining locked in its cage, especially if it is someday passed on to another owner.

Whatever method you choose, always use positive reinforcement. Negative reinforcement simply does not work (if it did, every child could be punished just once and behave admirably for the rest of its life). Never, no matter what the circumstances, strike a parrot. It will always remember the incident, and it will lose its trust and confidence in you.

Training

Whatever species you select, consider obtaining a young bird. Young birds are easier to tame, to teach to talk, and they usually have a more trusting disposition, especially when handfed. However, young birds that have not been handfed can still be easy to train. Even older birds can be trained, although it requires a lot more time and patience. Some parrots that have been in multiple homes may, through no fault of their own, come with their own emotional baggage or problems. These birds are more of a challenge, especially if you are a new owner. Newly weaned baby parrots that are ready for placement in new homes are much more receptive to training and interacting with a new family.

Wing Clipping

It is not uncommon to clip a bird's wings to help facilitate the taming process. However, wing clips should not be so severe that they impair the bird's physical appearance or create danger to the

A juvenile Blue and Gold macaw learns to step up to its owner, one of the first things taught in training.

bird itself. By clipping feathers too short, a bird could beat its wings against the bars while inside the cage, causing blood feathers (live feathers filled with blood) to form. If an owner is unfamiliar with blood feathers, it is best to bring the bird to a qualified avian veterinarian who will correctly pull the feather to stop the flow of blood. An active blood feather is considered a life-threatening emergency and a bird should be rushed to its veterinarian for proper treatment or it could bleed to death. For this reason, wing clipping should only be performed by an experienced bird handler or avian veterinarian.

Wing clipping is similar to getting a haircut and does not hurt the bird. However, wing clipping can be traumatic for an older bird or a very wild parrot that is not accustomed to being restrained in a towel. It is best to enlist the help of someone to hold the bird and a second individual to perform the actual clip so that the event is not associated with you.

There are several opinions on which type of wing clip works the best. One popular method is to cut most of the secondary flight feathers plus the primary feathers on each wing, leaving the outer two or three primary feathers intact. This cut will enable the bird to fly in a downward straight line, allowing the outer primary feathers to break its fall. For wilder birds, or strong fliers like cockatiels, it is usually necessary to cut the outer primaries so the bird is completely unable to fly and more amenable to hand taming.

Taming

There are two basic methods to taming. The first is the natural method of working to gain your parrot's trust and confidence by being patient, gentle, and nonthreatening. This is achieved by taking the "parrot's point of view," theoretically exchanging places with your bird and attempting to understand how your parrot views you and the world around it.

Begin by talking gently and soothingly to your parrot, and allow your hand to linger near the cage. Eventually, offer a favorite food such as a peanut or sunflower seed through the bars of the cage. The idea is to associate your hand with a positive food reward.

The next stage is to allow your hand to linger by the opened cage door while you routinely change the feed and water. Try to offer a favorite morsel of food from your hand. If your parrot is frightened, back off for now and return to an earlier step. But, do not give up; try to return to this step the next day. Once your parrot appears comfortable with your hand in the cage and is accepting delicious morsels of food, try to coax the bird onto your finger(s) by moving them ever so slowly

Training and Taming

Wing clipping, an important part of training, should be done with scissors pointed away from a bird's body, to prevent injury.

toward the bird's abdomen and gently pushing up under the breast to force it off balance. The parrot will then immediately step onto your finger. Repeat this procedure over the next few days.

Finally, move the bird outside the cage while it is still on your finger. Keep still and talk soothingly, cooing to it in soft, positive tones of encouragement. Reward your bird if you wish with a food treat. You can continue this procedure until your parrot is trained to ride on your shoulder, sit on a playstand, or learn other behaviors. This type of training is best suited to very young parrots newly weaned, or handfed babies that may step onto your hand right away but need to get to know you and build a special bond.

The second method of training is control training or force training. It is a popular method for older parrots that have not been tamed, or wilder parrots that are frightened of people. In this method, a wing clip is absolutely necessary.

Some bird behaviorists recommend taking the parrot into a small room such as a bathroom with all mirrors covered, windows and doors locked, and the toilet seat down. Allow the parrot to come out of the cage and slowly attempt to get the bird to step up onto your arm. The parrot, no doubt, will attempt to run away. However, after a time, your parrot will become so exhausted running around that it will climb up onto your arm if it is offered in a calm, reassuring manner. You can offer your parrot a perch initially, but if a perch is used for a prolonged period of time you could end up with a stick-trained, rather than a hand-trained parrot.

Should your parrot attempt to bite you, curl your hand into a fist so that it cannot easily inflict any real injury. Your parrot is at a critical stage of training and if it senses your fear, anger, or disappointment, it will react to it. Should your parrot attempt to bite out of fear, try not to jump or react, which tells the parrot it is succeeding in frightening you away. Once again, new owners are

Once a bird is tamed, it may feel comfortable enough to ride around on your shoulder as you go about your household business.

encouraged to acquire only younger or handfed birds that will respond more easily to taming.

Always behave gently and lovingly, with slow decisive movements, and talk encouragingly to your parrot. Reward your parrot with a food treat once it is on your arm or pair the food with the words, "Good bird!" Eventually, all the reward your bird will need is to hear you exclaim, "Good bird!"

The next step is to teach your bird a series of behavioral commands such as "Up," when you wish your bird to step up onto your hand; "Down," when you wish your bird to step back down onto its perch; or "No!" if your bird is attempting to bite you or engages in undesirable behavior. State these commands calmly without shouting and pair them at the moment your bird performs the exact behavior. Reward your bird with either a food reward or social reward such as "Good bird!" If you state an emphatic "No" when your parrot does attempt to nip you, immediately reward its very next behavior (e.g. such as stepping back on its playstand) with "Good bird!" so that the reinforcement is accentuating the positive rather than the negative.

Teaching to Talk

Undoubtedly, some species of parrots have a better reputation for learning how to talk than others. Psittacines such as African Greys, Yellow-naped Amazons, Double Yellow-headed Amazons, and Blue-fronted Amazons are the most talented, although almost all parrots can learn to say at least a few words. In this case, the talent lies with the teacher and not just with the pupil.

In general, it is easier to teach a parrot to talk once it has become tame and trustful of its owner. One person should be in charge of training so as not to confuse the bird with different voice pitches and tones. Once the bird begins to speak, it can be remarkably effective to mimic back the parrot's voice so it recognizes the precise pitch. For some unexplained reason, many parrots are more inclined to mimic female voices rather than male voices.

Start with a one- or two-word phrase and repeat it over and over. Popular phrases such as "Good bird" or "Pretty bird" are easily picked up because of their many soft consonants

Helpful Hint

Parrots use their beak as a third "hand" while climbing. It is perfectly normal for them to gently hold your fingers with their beak, prior to stepping up onto your hand. Don't ruin your training by yanking your hand back and sending confusing signals to your parrot.

Training and Taming

rather than vowels. Set up a regular schedule for daily lessons. Keep in mind that parrots have limited time spans, so lessons should not go much beyond 10 to 15 minutes. One option is to purchase training tapes as an adjunct to your personal lessons or record your own training tape. Start with a morning lesson before leaving for work, followed up by playing a training tape upon your arrival home. Once you've eaten dinner and are more relaxed, present the third lesson that you can enjoy together.

The average time to learn how to talk can vary, so be patient and don't give up. Once the first word is uttered, it is generally easier to learn future words. Eventually, everything will come pouring out and learning will then become much easier and much more rapid. A final warning, be careful what you repeat in front of your bird! Don't teach your parrot any bad habits. In some cases it only takes that one time, and you'll hear that embarrassing phrase time and again.

Although treats can be used as rewards during training, praise and attention can be just as fulfilling.

Behavior

No parrot guide would be complete without addressing a few of the idiosyncrasies peculiar to parrot behavior. Although some of these behaviors are quite normal, others may be signs of more problematic situations. With patient study, the acute observer can quickly learn to understand a parrot's "hidden language" and routine habits, then head off warning signs of larger problems.

Normal Behavior

Many new parrot owners are perplexed by behaviors that are perfectly normal in parrots.

Beak Grinding

Healthy birds engage in beak grinding, the sound of grating their top and lower mandibles together, particularly when they are preparing to roost for the night. It is thought that beak grinding might be the birds' method of trimming their own beaks by grinding down growing layers to prevent overgrowth.

Standing on One Leg

Another puzzling sign to new owners is a parrot standing on one leg, oftentimes while napping or sleeping. This is healthy, because if the bird were sick it would require both feet to perch to keep its balance. Another unique sleep behavior is when a parrot tucks its head into its wing, actually placing its beak into its back feathers, which is the preferred position for healthy psittacines.

Odds and Ends

Another odd behavior is when a bird grasps food in one claw while eating, a behavior that varies from individual to individual. An often perplexing behavior is when birds hang upside down or rightside up with wings spread open, indicating they'd appreciate a bath or a rain shower. Finally,

Some abnormal behaviors are easy to detect, such as this extreme case of feather plucking.

wing beating, especially while inside the cage, simply indicates the need for exercise or flight.

Abnormal Behavior

Some concerns of new parrot owners border on health issues. Signs of the following behaviors should be noted and discussed with an avian veterinarian.

Begging Behavior

If a young parrot starts to make whining or begging sounds, frequently accompanied by head-bobbing, chances are it may not be fully weaned. Contact the seller immediately to get further instructions should you need to continue feeding. On occasion, a weaned baby parrot will continue to beg for an easy meal, but it should be able to feed itself and fill its crop full each night. If it does not, contact a professional immediately.

Sneezing and Yawning

Many new owners wonder if it is normal for parrots to occasionally sneeze, or even repeatedly yawn. Birds may occasionally sneeze, which can be attributed to dust (especially in species with more powder down like cockatiels and cockatoos), just as a person would sneeze if exposed to an irritant. If the bird keeps sneezing repeatedly, or shows pink or red nostrils, then seek medical attention. Yawning is often the act of a bird popping its ear canals, and there is no harm in an occasional yawn. However, continuous yawning could indicate a sinus or upper respiratory problem.

Feather Plucking

Some parrot owners are concerned about whether their parrot is feather plucking or engaging in normal preening activities. As a parrot preens its feathers it uses its beak to "comb" each feather individually, tuck in and smooth out feathers, and apply oil to its feathers from the oil gland found above the tail. There should not be bare patches on the body, although it is not unusual to find a few small body feathers or an occasional flight or tail feather on the cage bottom when going through a molt.

On the other hand, feather plucking reveals bare patches of skin or rough feathering on the chest and sometimes the body, usually with many feathers found at the cage bottom. Some birds even rub their head and face against cage bars.

Birds that carry bald spots that are exceptions to the above include the lutino and fallow mutation cockatiels, with its inherited bald spot behind the crest, or birds that pull feathers to line their nests because they wish to breed. When one parrot has access to another parrot and one of the birds is missing head or face feathers, it usually indicates that the bird's companion is doing the honors.

Feather plucking should be taken seriously, because if left unchecked some parrots have been known to severely injure or kill themselves with self-inflicted wounds. The first step is to take the bird in for a veterinary checkup. The second step is to feed the bird a nutritional diet. The third step is to provide a stimulating environment that includes an appropriate size cage, safe toys, time outside the cage, and companionship

Behavior

from people or other birds. If none of the above work, contact a professional bird behaviorist.

Foot Attacking Syndrome

Another dangerous syndrome, and one that is especially known to affect Amazon parrots, is foot biting syndrome. This unfortunate syndrome occurs when hormone levels rise and remain high, resulting in a frustrated parrot that takes its mounting aggression out by attacking its own foot. Some merely pretend to bite while yelling. In more serious cases, real damage can result. Evaluate the environment and attempt to divert the behavior or seek a behavior therapist. If possible, a breeding loan program might be worth considering should all else fail.

Occasional biting is normal, such as when a bird is threatened, but aggressive and regular biting is a problem.

Transferred Aggression

During breeding season many parrots that were formerly sweet and tame can suddenly turn hostile and bite their owners. Do not take it personally—your parrot merely wishes to breed, and some parrots, when threatened in a captive situation, are known to attack their mates out of a frustrated need to guard their territory or nest. In this situation you are viewed as either the mate or the intruder. This reaction is simply the result of hormones, and your parrot will return to its lovable self when hormones return to normal levels. Don't take any unnecessary chances such as putting your face within easy reach.

Screaming

Some parrots learn how to annoy their owners by screaming. Screaming can be a learned behavior that enables a parrot to get what it wants or needs. Most often, it is a legitimate request that its owner is simply not aware of: parrots may scream if they do not receive their food on schedule, if they are confined to their cage, or if they are denied your company. A parrot's needs should always be met.

However, screaming can sometimes be instigated by other causes, such as an over-stimulating environment; lamp lights left on after bedtime; loud music, television, or other noise; or other birds, animals, or people.

Some birds respond to simply having a cover placed over the cage. The cover signals bedtime and quiet time and may be all that is needed. Soothing music (e.g. gentle classical, soft rock, etc.) can even quiet a ranting pet. Fast or hard rock music will only further stimulate your bird.

Finding a Bird Behaviorist

In most instances, when you observe strange behavior or behaviors that are of concern to you, you should first contact your avian veterinarian and ask if you need to schedule an appointment. Many times, an underlying medical condition can cause a behavior. If illness is ruled out and you have tried other alternatives, it may be time to contact a professional bird behaviorist. Ask your veterinarian for a referral or search through any of the bird specialty magazines carried in pet stores. Don't let a problem go. Your bird depends upon you.

Health Care

Providing quality health care is key to maintaining your parrot in optimum condition. Keeping a regular schedule, including feeding, bathing, and bedtime, is paramount to a healthy lifestyle. Annual veterinary exams can be just as important to your parrot's health. Such exams can include regular nail trims and wing clips, if desired; exams may identify underlying health conditions before they get out of hand. As owners of our companion birds, it is up to us to provide them with the care they deserve.

Bathing

Most parrots enjoy bathing and will attempt to bathe in their water dishes if deprived of the activity. Species from the tropical rainforest enjoy "rain showers"; those from more arid regions usually enjoy rolling in soaking wet greens as they would in the wild after a rainfall.

All parrots can be trained to enjoy a light misting from a plant atomizer. Fill the atomizer with warm, plain water and spray a gentle mist up in the air over the bird so it falls lightly down on its head. Eventually, your parrot will respond by opening its wings, twisting and hanging upside down to receive the spray over its wings and back. Never use the atomizer for anything else or put any other substances in it. Some birds enjoy accompanying their owner into the shower; there are even special shower perches that can be attached in the shower for your bird. Bathe your birds frequently in hot weather and less frequently in cooler weather. If there is a draft or it is too close to bedtime, skip the bath.

Schedules

Keeping your bird on a regular schedule will help it remain healthy. Consistent schedules reduce stress and provide a dependable environment for your bird. Try to feed your bird at the same time

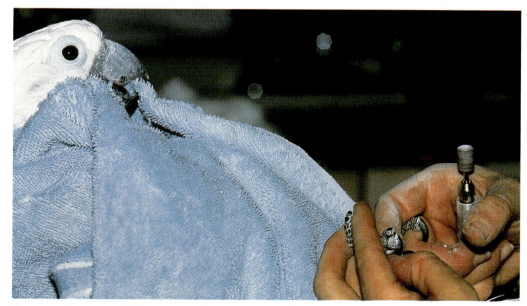
Periodic nail trimming will help to prevent future foot problems from developing.

each day, maintain a regular cleaning schedule, and most importantly, stick to a routine bedtime so your parrot gets its rest. If you must stay up reading late, turn off the light for your bird and go into another room. When traveling with your parrot, try and keep as normal a schedule as is possible.

Preventive Care

Be prepared and keep a first-aid kit on hand. Your kit should include bandages, blood-stop to stop bleeding, nail trimmers, leg band cutters, handfeeding syringes (for medications), and any other materials your veterinarian suggests you should have on hand. It is also useful to invest in a gram scale so that you are able to keep track of your bird's weight and report any significant changes to your veterinarian.

In nearly every situation, the first step in first aid is to apply heat. Heat will allow your bird to stay warm so that it has the strength to eat (offer your bird its favorite soft foods at this time) and fight off infection.

You may wish to invest in a hospital cage, or construct a makeshift cage yourself. If assembling your own hospital cage, you will need to purchase a second smaller cage, because large cages rarely retain the heat.

Place a heating pad under the grid in the cage tray and cover with newspaper. Wrap all sides, including the top and the lower front of the cage, with several layers of towels and blankets, tightly tucked in, leaving only the upper front half of the cage unwrapped. The idea is to heat the cage gradually up to 85 to 90 degrees Fahrenheit. Be certain to keep any wires out of reach. Another possibility is to use a bird carrier or acrylic cage with holes for ventilation.

Whatever you use, check the cage frequently to make sure it is the correct temperature. Birds that are too cold sit fluffed up. Birds that are too hot hold their wings out at the shoulders and open their beaks in an effort to cool down. Applying heat in time can save a bird's life. When traveling to the veterinarian, unplug the heating pad and place the entire unit in a deep carton and cover it up to contain the heat. Once at the clinic, uncover the top, plug in the heating pad, and turn it back on so your bird can continue to stay warm. A second alternative is to place the bird in a pet carrier, lined with a soft towel, with spray millet and an orange slice for the journey, then cover it securely with many towels.

Avian Veterinary Visits

If possible, locate an avian veterinarian who is board certified or a veterinarian who specializes in birds. The veterinary visit will usually consist of a physical exam where the parrot is secured in a towel while the veterinarian palpates the breastbone, listens to the heart and lungs, and examines the body for lumps and other problems. The oral cavity (mouth), eyes, nares (nostrils), and beak are checked with a pen light; the bird is weighed; and a history is taken of the bird, including recent symptoms. If warranted, further tests are ordered, including (but not limited to) a gram stain, cloacal culture, and a blood chemistry profile. If necessary, additional tests for chlamydia, polyomavirus, and Psittacine Beak and Feather Disease can be ordered.

Bird Rescue

Although it may be tempting to take in a parrot in need of a home, be certain that you put it through regular quarantine procedures to protect your other birds. Birds that are abandoned or given up aren't always in the best of health and should be brought in for an avian exam before introducing them to your other birds.

Whenever considering adopting or buying another bird, find out its complete history. Try and stay in touch with the original owners if you can in case you need further information. Many bird clubs run successful adoption programs and have very specific guidelines. If you are seeking to adopt a parrot, you will need to be a member of the bird club running the program. Many of the more than 200 bird clubs around the country are listed in the specialty bird magazines carried in pet stores. The Gabriel Foundation, a nonprofit organization dedicated to the education of the public and bird rescue, places many parrots every year (see Resources).

Responsibility

Learn all you can about taking the best possible care of your parrot. He is your special friend and relies solely on you. Purchase books on the particular species, subscribe to one of the specialty magazines devoted to parrots, and make an effort to attend one of the numerous avicultural conventions that educate parrot owners on how to take better care of their birds. Such conventions have top national speakers, large exhibit halls filled with beneficial parrot-related merchandise, and can update attendees on important medical research and conservation efforts that will benefit our birds both in captivity and in the wild.

Resources

AFA Watchbird
American Federation of Aviculture, Inc.
P.O. Box 56218
Phoenix, AZ 85079
www.afa.birds.org
The AFA is a nonprofit organization dedicated to the promotion of aviculture and the conservation of avian wildlife through the encouragement of captive breeding programs, scientific research, and the education of the general public. The AFA publishes a bi-monthly magazine called *AFA Watchbird*.

Association of Avian Veterinarians
P.O. Box 811720
Boca Raton, FL 33481
561-393-8901
www.aav.org
AAV membership is comprised of veterinarians from private practice, zoos, universities and industry; veterinary educators, researchers and technicians; and veterinary students. Serves as resource for bird owners who are looking for certified avian veterinarians.

Bird Talk
Subscription Dept.
P.O. Box 57347
Boulder, CO 80323
www.animalnetwork.com
Bird Talk is a monthly magazine noted for its directory of avian breeders, as well as its species profiles and informative articles and columns on health care and behavior.

Bird Times
Pet Publishing, Inc.
7-L Dundas Circle
Greensboro, NC 27407
www.birdtimes.com
Bird Times is a source of entertaining and authoritative information about birds. Articles include bird breed profiles, medical reports, training advice, bird puzzles, and personal stories about special birds.

The Gabriel Foundation
P.O. Box 11477
Aspen, CO 81612
www.thegabrielfoundation.org
The Gabriel Foundation is a nonprofit organization promoting education, rescue, adoption, and sanctuary for parrots.

The NAPS Journal
North American Parrot Society, Inc.
P.O. Box 404
Salem, OH 44460
www.drzoolittle.com/napshome.htm
NAPS members are individual pet owners, breeders with small and large aviaries, show judges, veterinarians, and people who enjoy exhibiting. Members can purchase closed bands from NAPS.

Index

African Grey 8, 14
African Ringneck 18
Age 7
"Alex" 14
Alexandrine 19
Amazon parrots 7, 8, 9
Australian parakeets 16
Avian veterinarian 61
Bandages 60
Baraband 16
Bare-eyed cockatoo 11
Bathing 59
Beak grinding 55
Bee Bee parakeet .21
Begging 56
Bird carrier 37
Bird rescue 62
Black-headed caique 21
Blood feather 50
Blood-stop 60
Blossom-head 19
Blue and Gold macaw 12
Blue-crowned conure 20
Blue-fronted Amazon 9
Blue-headed 20
Bourke's parakeet 16
Bronze-wing 20
Brown-head 18
Budgerigar 22, 23
Cage cleaning 38
Cage covers 35
Cage safety 34
Cage size 11, 12, 33
Caiques 21
Calcium 46
Canary-winged parakeet 21
Cape 18
Chattering 16
Citron cockatoo .11
Closed band 28
Cockatiels 17
Cockatoo .7, 8, 10
Congo African Grey 15
Conures 20
Crimson rosella 16
Derbyan parakeet 19
Diet 27
Double Yellow-headed Amazon 9
Droppings 26
Eastern rosella 16

Eclectus parrots .15
Extruded diets 42
Feather condition 24
Feather plucking .56
Feather-picking 43
Foot attacking syndrome 57
Galah 11
Glaucous macaw .13
Goffin's cockatoo .11
Golden Mantled rosella 16
Grand Eclectus 15
Greater Rose-ringed parakeet 19
Greater Sulphur-crested cockatoo 11
Green-rumped parrotlet 23
Green-winged macaw 12
Grey-cheeked parakeet 21
Hahn's macaw 14
Handfeeding syringes 60
Hospital cage 60
Hyacinth macaw .13
Identification .8, 27
Illiger's macaw 14
Illness 26
Indian Ringneck .18
Jardine parrot 18
Jenday conure 20
Leadbeater 11
Lear's macaw 13
Leg band 8
Lesser Sulphur-crested cockatoo 11
Lilacine Amazon .10
Lories 16
Lorikeets 16
Lovebirds 22
Macaw 7, 8, 11
Major Mitchell's cockatoo 11
Maroon-bellied conure 20
Masked lovebird .22
Maximilian's 20
Meyers parrot 18
Microchip 29
Military macaw 13
Mimicking ability 14
Minerals 42, 46
Mini-macaws 13
Molting 24
Moluccan cockatoo 10
Moustache parakeet 19
Nail trimmers 60
Noble macaw 14

Index

Noise 12	Slateyhead 19
Orange-winged Amazon 9	Sleep behavior .55
Pacific parrotlet 23	Sneezing 56
Parrot pellets 42	Solomon Island Eclectus 15
Parrotlets 22, 23	Source 7
Peachface lovebird 22	Spectacled parrotlet 23
People food 43	Stanley rosella 16
Pepperberg, Dr. Irene 14	Sulphur-crested cockatoo 10
Perches 34	Sun conure 20
Personality 8	Sunflower seeds 42
Playstands 36	Table food 43, 44
Plumhead parakeets 19	Talking 52
Prescription diets 42	Taming 50
Princess of Wales 16	Timneh African Grey 15
Quaker parakeets 21	Toys 10, 37
Quarantine .30, 31	Training 49
Queen of Bavaria conure 20	Transferred aggression 57
Rainbow lorikeet 16	Umbrella cockatoo 10, 11
Red lory 16	Vegetables .43, 44
Red-bellied 18	Vitamin A 44, 46
Red-headed conure 20	Vitamin K 46
Red-lored Amazon 9	Vitamins 42, 46
Red-rump parakeet 16	Vosmaeri Eclectus 15
Red-sided Eclectus 15	Water 46
Regent parrot 16	Weaning 29
Ringneck parakeet 18	Weight 27
Rock Pebbler 16	Western rosella .16
Rose-breasted cockatoo 11	White-breasted caique 21
Rosellas 16	White-capped 20
Scarlet macaw .12	White-eared conure 20
Schedules 59	White-fronted Amazon 10
Screaming .10, 57	Whole grain rice 44
Seed mixes 41	Wing clipping 49
Senegal parrot .18	Yawning 56
Severe macaw .14	Yellow-collared macaw 14
Sex 8	Yellow-naped Amazon 9
Sexually dimorphic 15	Yellow-thighed caique 21
Size 7	

Photo Credits

Joan Balzarini: 16, 21, 22, 27, 30, 31, 36, 43, 44, 46
Isabelle Francais: 4, 6, 8, 14, 19, 23, 29, 32, 34, 37, 38, 42, 51, 52, 58
Michael Gilroy: 17B, 53, 57
Robert Pearcy: 54, 56
Ronald Smith: 35
John Tyson: 9, 10, 12, 13, 15, 17T, 18, 24, 50